Academic English

Academic English
Skills for Success

Letty Chan   Louisa Chan   Miranda Legg   Wai Lan Tsang

香港大學出版社
Hong Kong University Press

Hong Kong University Press
14/F Hing Wai Centre
7 Tin Wan Praya Road
Aberdeen
Hong Kong
www.hkupress.org

© Hong Kong University Press 2012

ISBN 978-988-8139-25-5

British Library Cataloguing-in-Publication Data
A catalogue record for this book is available from the British Library.

10 9 8 7 6 5 4 3 2 1

Printed and bound by Liang Yu Printing Factory, Ltd., Hong Kong, China

Contents

Unit 4

China and Asia: Synthesizing your own and others' ideas for your assignments 103

Unit 5

Values: Structuring texts for your assignments 135

Unit 6

Editing your written assignments 161

Acknowledgements

Many people have contributed to this textbook in various ways.

The authors specifically wish to thank the following:

The University of Hong Kong for the Teaching Development Grant which funded the writing of this textbook.

The staff at the Centre for Applied English Studies at the University of Hong Kong who helped to pilot the early versions of these materials and gave invaluable feedback.

The students who also generously gave feedback on the early versions of the materials.

Professor Ken Hyland, Professor Agnes Lam, Dr David Gardner and Eliza Yu, who have given guidance along the way.

Introduction for students

Aims

This course aims to:

- develop the **general (not discipline-specific) academic English skills** you **will** need to complete your undergraduate degree at university and
- help you make the transition from secondary school study to study at an English-medium university.

Learning outcomes

By the end of the course you should be able to:

- **communicate ideas and data** related to academic topics in a clear and structured way, using academic sources;
- **argue for an opinion (a stance)** in a clear and structured way, using academic sources;
- **produce three common spoken** and **written academic texts**: an essay, a report and a tutorial discussion;
- **form a stance** about academic topics through critical reading; and
- **write and speak English** using appropriate grammar and vocabulary.

How to make the most of this textbook

1. Apply skills practised in this textbook to your other courses

Through the textbook you are asked to apply the skills you have learnt to other courses you are currently taking. The work you do in this textbook should be useful in many, if not all, of your university courses. The application tasks will also require you to read authetnic texts and texts you choose for yourself. We hope this is motivating for you!

2. Participate actively

By the end of the course you will have practised academic writing, read a number of academic texts, and participated in a series of academic speaking tutorials. You will get the most out of these tasks if you participate actively in and out of class.

3. Do complementary work

Your teacher will supplement the work in this textbook with other work on grammar, vocabulary, citation and referencing skills and tasks on how to avoid plagiarism. This work is very important and will help you to achieve the aims listed above.

Textbook map

Units	1	2	3	4	5	6
Unit Focus	Introduction to university writing and speaking	Gathering information for your assignments	Finding and expressing your stance for your assignments	Synthesizing your own and others' ideas for your assignments	Structuring texts for your assignments	Editing your written assignments
Unit Overview	Identifying features of academic writing and course overview	Analysing assignment topics in preparation for reading	Using the language of expressing stance; using the evidence for expressing stance	Writing cohesive paragraphs in academic writing	Structuring academic texts	Understanding the editing process
Reading	Identifying good sources of academic information	Gathering information using textual signals	Recognizing and understanding stance while reading	Identifying main ideas and supporting details	Evaluating ideas and data in a text	Analysing the weaknesses of a written assignment
Grammar	Identifying and correcting common areas of weakness	Linking words for expressing similarities and contrast	Hedging	Using pronouns in paragraph structure	Using linking words and phrases	Proofreading
Writing	Exploring the academic writing process	Note-taking and paraphrasing	Writing good topic sentences	Synthesizing ideas when writing paragraphs	Writing a well-structured text	Editing and rewriting
Vocabulary	Understanding collocation	Citation in tutorial discussions	Choosing appropriate vocabulary to show your stance	Describing data and trends	Signposting in tutorial discussions	**Self-assessment**
Speaking	Exploring academic speaking	Transforming written language into spoken language	Expressing your stance in tutorial discussions	Describing data and trends	Responding to opposing arguments	**Self-assessment**
Speaking tutorial	Supporting opinions and discussing complexity	Transforming written language into spoken language	Understanding the importance of questioning in tutorial discussions	Integrating data to support your stance	Summary	**Self-assessment**

Introduction to university writing and speaking

Test your knowledge

Answer these questions about Unit 1 with your partner.

1. What types of speaking and writing assignments will you be expected to do while you are studying for your degree?

2. What are some common areas of grammar that are difficult for English as a second language university students?

3. What skills do you need to participate in a tutorial discussion?

Learning outcomes

By the end of this unit, you should be able to:

- understand the basic features of academic writing and speaking at university level;
- understand the academic writing process;
- identify good sources of academic information for completing written and spoken assignments;
- identify common areas of grammar that are difficult for Hong Kong students;
- understand what collocation is;
- identify collocations using concordancers and dictionaries; and
- support opinions in a tutorial discussion from reading.

Overview of Unit

Identifying features of academic writing and course overview

This textbook will help you develop many of the academic English communication skills needed to complete your written and spoken assignments at university.

The following table shows some common types of text that university students are expected to be able to complete.

Task 1
Identify academic texts you have written

Look at the different types of written and spoken texts in the box below. Put a tick next to the ones that you would feel confident completing right now. Compare your answers with those of the person next to you. Take five minutes to do this.

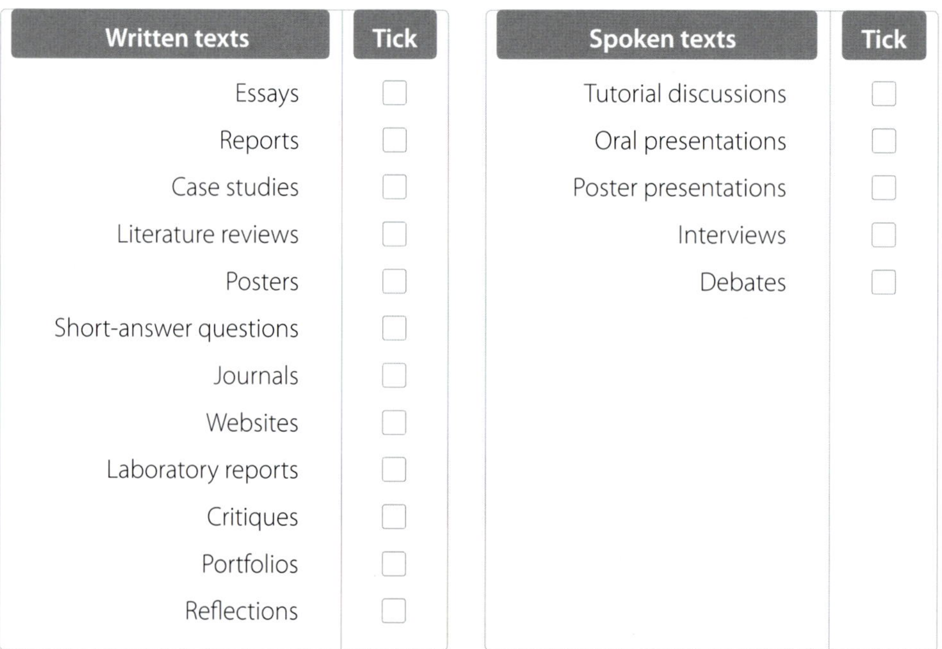

Written texts	Tick		Spoken texts	Tick
Essays	☐		Tutorial discussions	☐
Reports	☐		Oral presentations	☐
Case studies	☐		Poster presentations	☐
Literature reviews	☐		Interviews	☐
Posters	☐		Debates	☐
Short-answer questions	☐			
Journals	☐			
Websites	☐			
Laboratory reports	☐			
Critiques	☐			
Portfolios	☐			
Reflections	☐			

Throughout this textbook, we will be looking at **three types of text** which are very common at university: **the essay**, **the report** and **the tutorial discussion**. The reasons for using these three types of text are:

- They are some of the most common types of texts which undergraduates need to complete.

- They are used in a variety of disciplines from humanities to science.

- Many of the skills you need to complete an essay, a report and a tutorial discussion can be used to complete the other texts listed in the table.

Identifying features of academic writing

Features of academic writing at university

At university, your written texts should generally:

– be formal in tone

– use a variety of grammatical structures and vocabulary accurately to express complex academic ideas

– be logically and clearly organized

– use citation and referencing to show where you are referring to the ideas of others

When you are writing an essay or report you usually need to:

– acknowledge and discuss the complexity of the topic

– compare and contrast different ideas and data on the topic from your reading

– use these ideas and data to support your personal opinion (stance) on the topic

– acknowledge the fact that there are often valid arguments which don't agree with your opinion

– make conclusions which are well argued, logical and realistic

You will practise these skills throughout this textbook.

In a moment you are going to read an essay about health care, written by a first-year university student. Before you do this, complete the following task.

Task 2
Give your opinion

Answer these questions with the person next to you. It should take you five minutes to do this.

1. Who pays for health care in your country? The public? The government? A mixture of both?

2. What do you think is the ideal system, private or public? Why?

3. What could be the effect on the society as a whole if the health-care system doesn't work well?

Task 3

Express your opinion (stance) in writing

Now, look at the following essay topic.

Who should pay for health care in the developed world, the government or the public?

Complete the sentence in the box below. Your sentence should:

- give your opinion (stance) on this topic
- justify this opinion

It should take you five minutes to do this.

> Health care in the developed world should be paid for by … because …

Task 4

Identify features of academic writing in a student's essay

Read Text A. Find examples of the previously mentioned features of academic writing above on page 3. Underline the examples in the text. Compare them with those of your partner. It should take you fifteen minutes to do this.

Text A: Student essay

The topic of who should pay for health care is highly controversial and very complex. A person's opinion on this topic is likely to be related to his or her political and ethical views. There are four major methods of funding health-care systems in the developed world. They are direct payment by the user, taxation from the public, national health insurance and private health insurance. If we look again at the topic (whether the government or the public should pay), we can divide these four methods into two categories, government-provided health care (through taxation and national insurance schemes) and public-(user-) paid system (private health insurance and direct payment by the user at the time of treatment). This essay discusses different possible models of health care and suggests an ideal working model for most developed countries, that a combination of the two categories is the best system.

Belief about who should pay for health care is correlated to economic status. The richer you are, the more likely you are to support a user-paid system (Chan 2004). 'The rich' feel that this gives them greater control over their health care. They are able to get higher-quality medical services than the government could pay for, and shorter waiting times for access to complicated treatments like surgery. However, if we look at the United States as an example, this is often not true. "Despite having the most costly health system in the world, the United States consistently underperforms on most dimensions of performance, relative to other countries, such as quality, access, efficiency and equality" (Davis et al. 2007: 34). Higher cost does not necessarily mean better quality. The other major argument for a user-paid system is that it is our responsibility to pay if we can afford to do so. Although we pay tax, that money is needed for a number of purposes such as education and building new infrastructure. One could argue that, if you are rich enough to pay for some health care, then you should. It is difficult to argue against this point of view.

However, one obvious benefit to the government paying is that poor people are provided with health care. If a large percentage of the population could not afford medical care, people living below the poverty line would be severely affected. They would become unproductive. Also, much research has shown that people who have constant access to health care generally live healthier lives and cost the medical system less overall than those who go to the doctor only in an emergency (Williams 2005; Emerson 2006). So, although one would think that a government-paid system would be more expensive, in the end it could be cheaper for the population as a whole. However, there are also negative aspects to a government-paid system. It is often politically unpopular (Smith 2001), as governments need to increase taxation as the population ages. It is difficult for governments to convince people that a mostly government-run system could be cheaper and more efficient. Politicians do not want to hurt their political careers by bringing in higher taxation.

If we accept that no single system is perfect, then it seems that a government-paid system keep added aspects of a user-paid system is the best. Ms Smith, consultant to the World Health Organization, says that a comparison of health-care systems in the developed world shows that, if there is "a government safety net for the poor and also a user-paid element which helps to fund the health care for poorer citizens, then there is no obvious difference in health outcomes across countries, regardless of how the combination of government verses user works" (WHO 2006: 34). This is what most developed countries have at the moment. It seems that the problem is getting the right balance between these two aspects and making the system as a whole work efficiently.

How to fund health care is a very complex problem, and it is clear that there is no perfect solution. Differing political and ethical views within a country mean that it is unlikely that a country will reach an agreement about the best model. It seems, though, that as long as two basic aspects are covered, that of access for the poor and the ability for the wealthier population to help pay for the less wealthy population, then the system is likely to achieve most of its goals. In the future, as the populations of countries age, governments in the developed world will need to work hard to try to establish an effective mix of a user- and a government-paid system.

References

Chan, K. (2004). The link between health care systems and economic status. *The Journal of Public Health* 2(24): 325–65.

Davis, C., C. Schoen, M. Schoenbaum, A. Doty, J. Holmgren, & K. Shea. (2007). An international update on the comparative performance of American health care. *The Journal of International Health Education* 1(12): 125–204.

Etc.

Throughout this textbook you will explore how to complete written and spoken assignments for your university courses. You will look at five steps in the writing process and four steps in the speaking process.

Task 5
Order the steps of the writing process

Put the following steps of the writing process in order by putting a number from 1 to 5 next to the step. It should take you five minutes to do this.

Step	Number
Finding and expressing your stance (opinion)	
Synthesizing your own and others' ideas	
Gathering information on the topic	
Editing your writing	
Structuring your writing	

Steps in the writing and speaking processes and the structure of this textbook

Step One: Gathering information on the topic

You have to analyse the topic of the assignment in order to understand what information you need to read. You then need to read academic texts, take notes and paraphrase the ideas and data from texts you read.

You will practise these skills in **Unit 2**.

Step Two: Finding and expressing your stance (opinion)

You need to form your own opinion or stance about the topic, based on the reading that you have done.

You will practise doing this in the writing and speaking parts of **Unit 3**.

Step Three: Synthesizing your own and others' ideas

You need to integrate your own stance with the ideas and data that you have gathered from your reading. You will practise doing this in speaking in tutorial discussions and in writing, through writing well-structured paragraphs.

You will do this in **Unit 4**.

Step Four: Structuring your writing

You need to structure written texts in the form of logically organized essays and reports, and in speaking in tutorial discussions.

You will practise this in **Unit 5**.

Step Five: Editing your writing

The final step of the writing process is to edit what you have written.

You will practise this skill in **Unit 6**.

The following graphic summarizes these steps.

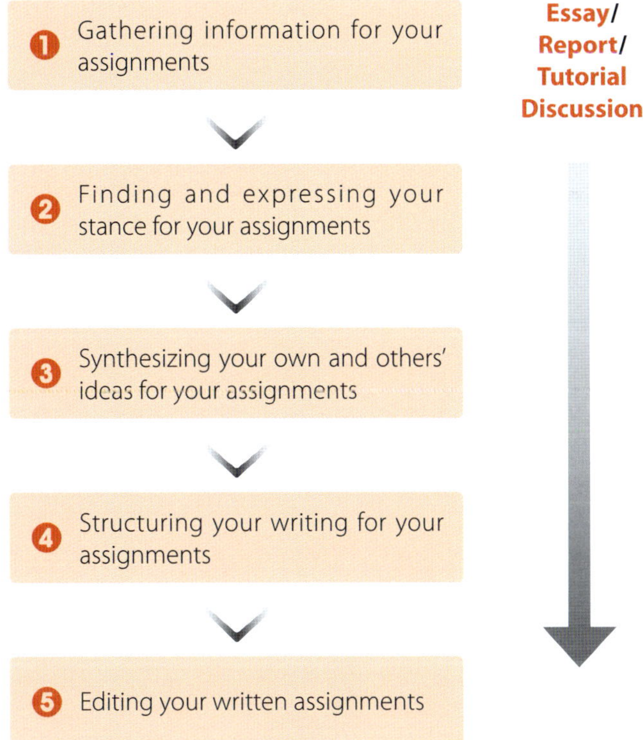

Task 6
Give your opinion

In a moment you are going to identify features of academic writing in a student's report in the same way as you did for the student's essay. Before you do that, however, look at the data in the following three graphics. Analyse them and decide what important information they show. Make some notes in the box below. Then compare your notes with those of your partner. Take ten minutes to do this.

Figure 1 Levels of obesity in Chinese aged 7–18

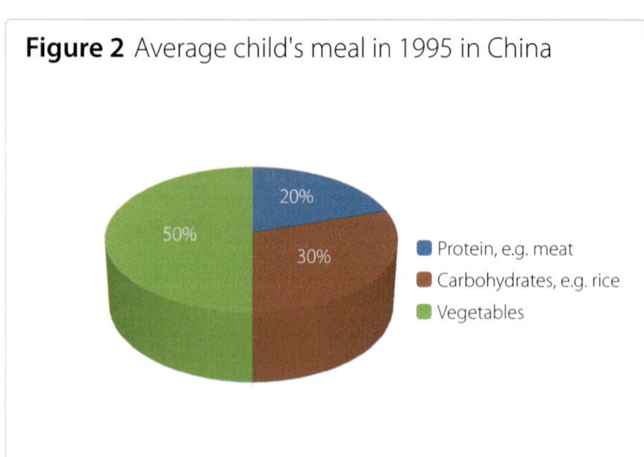

Figure 2 Average child's meal in 1995 in China

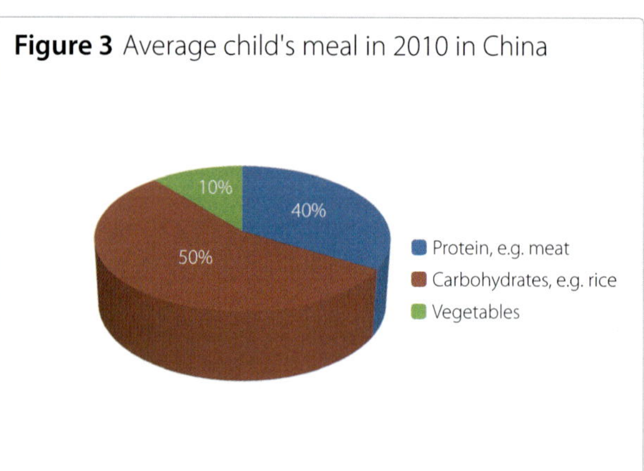

Figure 3 Average child's meal in 2010 in China

Homework

Identify features of academic writing in a student's report

Now, read Text B. See if you can find examples of the features of academic writing mentioned on page 3. Highlight the examples in the text. It should take you fifteen minutes to do this.

The topic of the report is:

How serious is the problem of childhood obesity in developing countries? What are the causes of it? What might be the solutions? Use the example of one developing Asian country to support your argument.

Text B: Student report

1. Summary

Childhood obesity in China is a serious problem, and it is getting increasingly worse. Levels of obesity are rising, slightly higher in boys than in girls. Diet is a big contributing factor, as well as lack of sleep and lack of exercise. A multifaceted approach is suggested to help alleviate the problem, including, for example, parents establishing a set bedtime for children and enforcing it, schools providing more time and motivation for students to exercise during and after school, and governments helping to improve education of students and parents about what a healthy meal should consist of.

2. Introduction

Obesity is now a very serious problem all around the world, increasingly for children as well as adults. Children these days are bombarded by advertisements telling them that they should be eating junk food rather than healthful food. Many play computer games rather than sports and stay up all night on the computer rather than getting a good night's sleep. The mass media and increasing materialism in society have a part to play in this phenomenon. All the habits mentioned above can lead to a child being overweight [1], and this can lead to lifelong physical problems such as diabetes, and psychological problems such as low self-esteem and depression. Research shows that if you are overweight as a child, you are more likely to be obese as an adult [2]. Much research has been done on the problem of childhood obesity in developed countries such as the United States of America and England; however, there has been less research in developing countries. So, how bad exactly is the problem in a rapidly developing country like China? The answer is that it is serious and becoming worse rather than improving with higher levels of education.

3. Levels of obesity

Levels of childhood obesity have been rising in China. Although the levels are significantly lower than the levels of being overweight, there has been a steady increase in both over the years. As boys are worse off than girls, the gap between boys and girls has been widening throughout the years.

3.1 Obesity in boys

The data show that the average weight for boys has been rising quite dramatically over the last 20 years (see Figure 1).

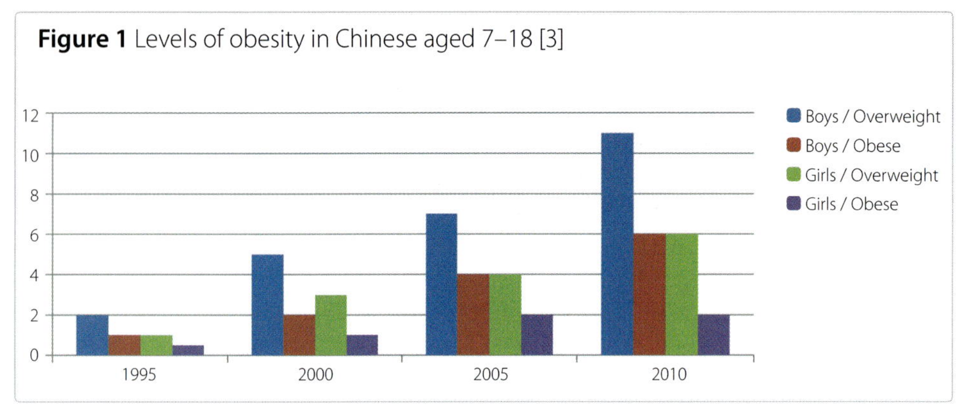

Figure 1 Levels of obesity in Chinese aged 7–18 [3]

In 1995, 2% of boys were overweight and 1% were obese. This figure rose to 5% and 2% respectively in 2000, 7% and 4% in 2005, and 11% and 6% in 2010.

3.2 Obesity in girls

One can see a similar pattern in girls as well. In 1995, 1% of girls were overweight and less than 1% were obese. In 2000, this rose slightly to 3% and 1% respectively. In 2005, the numbers were 4% and 2%, and in 2010, they were 6% and 2%.

Overall, these figures are in line with those in other developing countries in Asia, such as Malaysia **[3]**, Indonesia **[4]** and Thailand **[5]**. They all show similar trends: being overweight is increasing and is higher in boys than in girls.

4. Diet

It is likely that some part of this increase in weight can be attributed to a poorer diet. This can be seen when we compare the composition of an average meal eaten by children in China in 1995 and in 2010 (see Figures 2 and 3). This can be done by analysing the ratio of protein to carbohydrates to vegetables eaten.

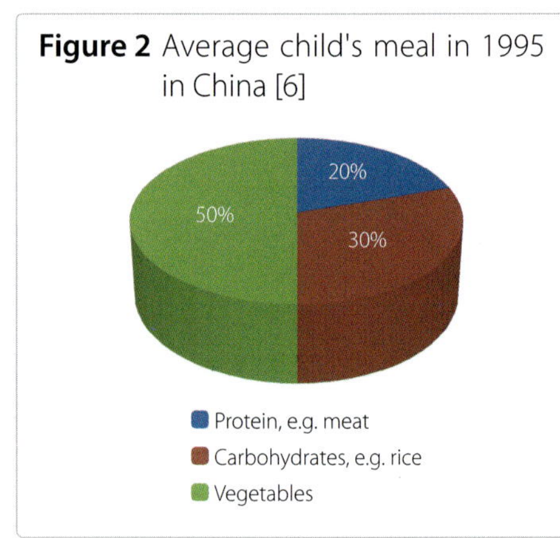

Figure 2 Average child's meal in 1995 in China [6]

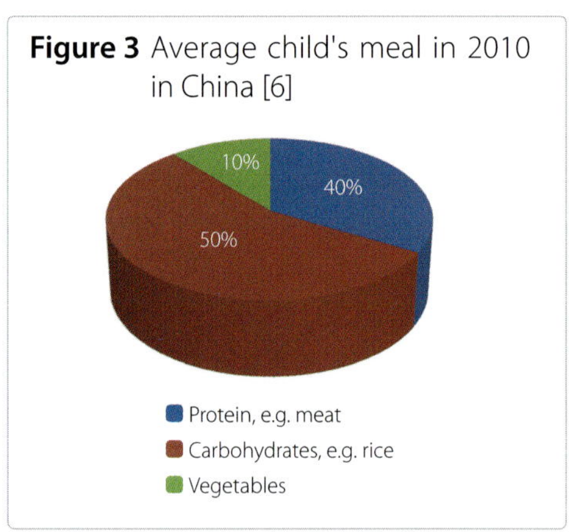

Figure 3 Average child's meal in 2010 in China [6]

4.1 Diet in 1995

In 1995, the average meal contained a 2:3:5 ratio of protein to carbohydrates to vegetables. Although this is a bit low in protein according to current thinking **[6]**, it has a good proportion of vegetables, which are high in nutrients and fibre but low in calories. It also has adequate carbohydrates, which will give a child enough energy for a day's activity.

4.2 Diet in 2010

If we look at the average meal in 2010, however, we can see that the ratios have changed quite dramatically. They are now 4:5:1, protein to carbohydrates to vegetables. The proportion of protein has doubled, and the proportion of vegetables has fallen to worryingly low levels. Most likely this diet is lacking in essential nutrients, and a child would be eating almost 100% to 200% more calories than a child in 1995, leading to significant weight gain over time.

It is clear that the average diet has become unhealthier over the years. It is likely that a child eating meals like this regularly would be lacking in nutrients and would be putting on a considerable amount of weight each year.

5. Other factors

The relationship of diet to weight is an important one, but it must be recognized that there are other factors influencing weight gain. Two areas which have been well-researched [7–12] are the amount of exercise and the amount of sleep, at least six hours a night. Research shows that both are correlated with weight gain. In China, 74% of secondary school students only do exercise when forced to at school, which only amounts to the equivalent of one and a half hours a week [7]. Primary students in China routinely get less than six hours sleep a night [7], often going to bed when their parents go to bed, which is often after midnight. The same problem can be seen in children in Indonesia [10] and Malaysia [11].

6. Possible solutions

Weight gain in children is a growing problem and is likely to increase in the future if parents and educators do not work towards helping children gain access to better-quality food, more time and opportunity to exercise and adequate sleep. There is no easy solution, as it involves issues related to culture, politics, education, government funding and problems arising from poverty. A multipronged approach seems to be the only solution. Schools, parents and governments must recognize the problem and take responsibility for it. Parents and governments need to ensure that children have access to good-quality, healthful food. Governments also need to educate students and parents as to what a healthy meal should consist of. Schools need to motivate children to exercise during and after school and give them a place in the curriculum to do this. Finally, parents also need to provide a quiet, relaxing environment for their children to sleep and set and enforce an appropriate bedtime.

References

1. Leung, M. L. (2008). Why are our children overweight? *The Journal of Public Health* 5(1): 39–60.
2. Philips, I. (2009). The link between child and adult obesity. *The Journal of Nursing* 2(5): 125–87.
Etc.

Academic Reading

Task 1
Give your opinion

Look at the list of health problems. All of these are serious health problems facing the developed world. Put them in order of seriousness, 1 being the most serious and 6 being the least serious. Compare your answers with those of your partner. Justify why your answers are right. Take ten minutes to do this task.

Health Problem	Number
Lack of work–life balance	
Pollution	
Increase in obesity	
Lack of access to high-quality and immediate health care	
Increase in viral diseases like H5N1	
Mental health problems like stress, anxiety and depression	

Task 2
Read for specific information

Imagine that you are writing an essay on the following topic:

Which health problem facing the developed world is currently the most serious?

You want to find information on the six problems you discussed in Task 1. You have found six texts, one on each problem. Read through the short texts. In the table below, make a note of any statistics or information showing the seriousness of each problem. Compare your answers with those of the person next to you. This task should take you fifteen minutes.

Health problem	Statistics showing the seriousness
Pollution	
Lack of work–life balance	
Increase in obesity	
Lack of access to high-quality and immediate health care for the poor	
Increase in viral illnesses like H5N1	
Mental health problems like stress, anxiety and depression	

Text 1

The Problem of the Work–Life Balance, by Sally Prince

Longer working hours, the high unemployment rate and lack of child care are just some of the barriers to a good work–life balance. In this book, Prince gathers data from interviews with mothers and fathers, employers and employees, all trying to balance working life and home life. Prince shows that the employment system in Australia and New Zealand has many systematic problems. She demonstrates that the lack of an affordable child care system leads to a loss of hundreds of millions of dollars from the economy in lost productivity, and she suggests a workable solution.

Text 2

About us

Courses

Students

Comments

Price list

Depression is an illness which affects the mind and body. Depression is experienced by people of all races and all cultures. Research estimates that more than 2.7 million people in the United Kingdom are currently suffering from depression. About 7,000 people commit suicide each year in the UK because of depression. Most people will experience depression at some time in their lives.

Since we began our company, we have helped thousands of people overcome depression by teaching them how to eat healthier and how to use meditation to relieve stress. We have also trained hundreds of people who work in the health care field. Currently we have about 1,500 students studying with us from around the world. Go to our comments page to see the messages from our many satisfied customers.

We currently offer over 20 courses on diet and lifestyle. We hope that you will join us and begin to lead a healthier life today.

If you are looking for anti-stress medication, look no further; go to www.medic.org today

"I never thought I would get rid of my depression, but GoSad worked and I now feel ready to take on the world!" (Mandy, 26, UK) To purchase GoSad, go to www.gosad.com today!

Text 3

Members

Statistics

The link between cancer and obesity

Considerable evidence shows that being overweight or obese plays an important role in the development of certain cancers.

About Us

The obesity group is a nonprofit scientific organization related to

<table>
<tr><td>

Education

Press

</td><td>

It has been clearly associated with a 200% increased risk of kidney cancer and a 150% increased risk of breast cancer in women. It seems that there is also a strong relationship between weight and colorectal cancer, gall bladder cancer and thyroid cancer in women. There is strong evidence from animal experiments that maintaining a healthy weight can delay the onset of many cancers. More research is needed to show whether this is true in humans as well.

</td><td>

research, prevention and treatment of obesity.

The society has 2,600 members, 50% of whom have a PhD, 32% are MDs and 14% are RDs. Members work in universities, hospitals, individual or group practice, medical schools, government and other fields.

The society publishes in peer-reviewed journals and holds a yearly international conference attended by over 1,000 medical professionals each year.

</td></tr>
</table>

Text 4

The Journal of Environmental Pollution, Volume 45, Number 2, pages 104–32

Air pollution and health, by Prof. John Duggan, PhD, and Prof. Levi Whitby, MD
School of Medicine, Southampton General Hospital, Southampton, UK

Summary

The health effects of air pollution have been the subject of extensive study in recent years. Exposure to pollutants has been associated with lower life expectancy (hypothesized to be possibly 2–3 years depending on the level of pollution) and admission to hospital as a result of respiratory and cardiovascular disease (about 3% of the population in heavily polluted cities). Negative health effects have also been seen at very low levels of exposure. In this article, the evidence for adverse effects on health of selected air pollutants is discussed.

Text 5

Wikipedia

Differences in access to health care in the United States

Reasons for differences in access to health care are many but can include the following:

- **Lack of insurance coverage.** Minority groups in the United States lack insurance coverage at higher rates than the majority Caucasian population. It is estimated that 19% of minority groups lack coverage, compared with 11.3% of Caucasians.

- **Structural barriers.** These barriers include poor transportation, an inability to schedule appointments quickly or during convenient hours, and excessive time spent in the waiting room, all of which affect a person's ability and willingness to obtain needed care.

This is especially problematic in rural areas, where the emergency room waiting time is 4.3 hours, compared to 2.4 hours in cities.

- **Linguistic barriers.** Medical care is difficult to access for those who do not speak English. They are reluctant to seek medical help if they fear there will be no one to translate for them.

Text 6

Los Angeles Times, Saturday, 25 July 2009

The worst-case scenario sees hundreds of thousands of deaths in the US from swine flu in the next two years, by John Williamson

Hundreds of thousands of Americans could die in the following years if a vaccine and other control measures for the new H1N1 influenza are not effective. The Center for Disease Control and Prevention (CDC) has also suggested that when the pandemic peaks, as much as 40% of the workforce could be affected.

Nineteen US states are now reporting widespread flu activity, mainly H1N1, according to Dr. John Schmidt, director of the CDC's National Center for Immunization and Respiratory Diseases. "That's very unusual at this time of year," he said. "This shows how easy it is to catch this type of virus."

Schmidt stated that in the last few months, 6% to 8% of the population in many US cities were infected by the virus even though it is not common to have figures like that in Spring. Now that the winter season is coming, "we think it will reach two to three times that number." Normally, 10% to 15% of people in a community are infected with seasonal flu.

Task 3
Evaluate sources of information

Look again at the texts. Think about whether they are good sources of information for a university student who is writing an academic essay or report. Why? Why not? Make notes in the table below. When you have finished, compare your answers with those of your partner. Justify your answers. Take ten minutes to do this task.

Text	Good source?	Reason
Text 1 – Book	☐ Yes ☐ No	
Text 2 – Website	☐ Yes ☐ No	

<table>
<tr><td>Text 3 – Website</td><td>☐ Yes ☐ No</td><td></td></tr>
<tr><td>Text 4 – Journal Article</td><td>☐ Yes ☐ No</td><td></td></tr>
<tr><td>Text 5 – Website</td><td>☐ Yes ☐ No</td><td></td></tr>
<tr><td>Text 6 – Newspaper article</td><td>☐ Yes ☐ No</td><td></td></tr>
</table>

Identifying good sources of academic information for your assignments

One important skill you will need throughout your university education is the ability to search for and select **good academic information**. You will not be able to complete your assignments without this skill.

How do you know whether a source of information is a good **academic** source?

Generally, information that has been through some kind of **editorial process** or has been **"fact-checked"** is reasonably reliable. These include:

- Books

- Journal articles (in print and online)

- Newspaper articles

Even though these sources have been through an editorial process, you still need to look for **bias** on the part of the author, especially in newspaper articles. You also want to think about the quality of journalism in the newspaper itself, whether it is part of the tabloid press.

Some other sources are also probably reliable although you can't be sure that they have been edited or fact-checked. These include:

- Government publications (in print and online)

- Publications (in print and online) of well-known organizations, e.g. The World Health Organization, The World Bank, Amnesty International

Again, you need to look for **biases**.

Lastly, there is the Internet. No one needs to go through any editorial process to publish information on a website. This is why you need to be **very careful** when you use information from a website.

When using an Internet source you should ask yourself the following questions:

1. **What is the purpose of the website?**

    – Advocacy (change opinion)

    – Commercial (sell a product or service)

    – Reference (provide access to information)

2. **Does the author have any qualifications related to the subject of the website?**

    Look for information in sections called something like "About us" or "Who we are".

3. **Does the content of the website show that the information is up-to-date?**

    Look for dates listed.

4. **Is the language used objective, or is it very emotional?**

    Emotional language can show that the writer is biased.

5. **Is the website linked to other well-known websites?**

    Do the authors link their website to other well-known websites?

Task 4
Re-evaluate sources of information

Now, look again at Task 3. Do you want to change your assessment now? Discuss this with your partner for five minutes.

Academic Grammar

The following activities introduce you to common problem areas of grammar for students when they are writing academic texts.

Task 1
Explore common areas of grammatical weakness

The following are eight common areas of grammatical weakness for students. Underline the errors in the incorrect sentences. Write the correct sentences in the column to the right. The first one has been done for you. Compare your answers with those of your partner. Tell your partner which of the eight areas are particularly difficult for you. This task should take you fifteen minutes.

Area of grammar	Incorrect sentences	Correct sentences
1. Countable/ Uncountable nouns	✗ There <u>have</u> been a lot of <u>researches</u> into obesity.	✓ There **has** been a lot of **research** into obesity.
	✗ Information on how to fight depression are available from the doctor.	✓
2. Articles (a/an/the is wrong, missing, or unnecessary)	✗ Pollution is serious problem in China.	✓
	✗ 6% to 8% of a population in many US cities were infected by the virus.	✓
3. Prepositions (wrong, missing, or unnecessary)	✗ Many researchers emphasize on how important exercise is.	✓
	✗ More research Is needed to show whether this is true on humans as well.	✓
4. Active/Passive voice	✗ The experiment carried out several times with the same result.	✓
	✗ Exposure to pollutants has associated with lower life expectancy.	✓

5. Participles present participle **~ing** past participle **~ed**	✗ 3% of the population are hospitalized for respiratory disease in heavily polluting cities.	✓
	✗ Go to our comments page to see the messages from our many satisfying customers.	✓
6. Tenses	✗ The health effects of air pollution were the subject of extensive study in recent years.	✓
	✗ Depression experienced by people of all races and all cultures.	✓
7. Singular/plural confusion	✗ Many of the worker were underpaid.	✓
	✗ In the last few month, the rate of infection has tripled.	✓
8. Sentence Structure (simple, complex, compound sentences)	✗ Although pollution is increasing in all parts of the developing world, but it is more serious in urban areas than in rural areas.	✓
	✗ Dr Scotts, he is the head of the flu pandemic taskforce at the Centre for Disease Control, states that there are more strains of flu this season than in previous years.	✓

Task 2
Proofread a text

Look at the first draft of two paragraphs from the student essay on health care. There are eight errors in this text, one from each of the eight categories listed above. Proofread the text for these errors, and correct the mistakes. Then compare your answers with those of your partner. This task should take you fifteen minutes.

Belief about who should pay for health care is correlating to economic status. The richer

you are, the more likely you are to support a user-paid system (Chan 2004). 'The rich' feel

that this gives them greater control for their health care. They are able to get higher-quality

medical services than the government could pay for, with shorter waiting times for access to complicated treatments like surgery. However, if we look at the United States as an example, this is often not true. "Despite having the most costly health system in the world, the United States consistently underperforms on most dimensions of performance, relative to other countries, such as quality, access, efficiency and equality" (Davis et al. 2007: 34). Higher cost does not necessarily mean better quality. The other major argument for a user-paid system is that it is in fact our responsibility to pay if we can afford to pay. Although we paid tax, that money is needed to go towards a lot of things such as education, building new infrastructure etc. One could argue that if you are rich enough to pay at least some money towards health cares, then you should. It is difficult to argue against this point of view.

However, one obvious benefit to the government paying is that the poor are provided with health care. If large percentage of the population could not afford medical care, people living below the poverty line would severely affected. They would become unproductive. Also, much research has shown that people who have constant access to health care generally live healthier lives and cost the medical system less overall, than those who only go to the doctor only in an emergency (Williams 2005; Emerson 2006). So, although one would think that a government-paid system would be more expensive, however in the end it could be cheaper for the population as a whole. However, there are also negative aspects to a government-paid system. It is often politically unpopular (Smith 2001), as government need to increase taxation as the population ages. It is difficult for governments to convince people that a mostly government-run system could be cheaper and more efficient. Politicians do not want to hurt their political careers by bringing in higher taxation.

Academic Writing

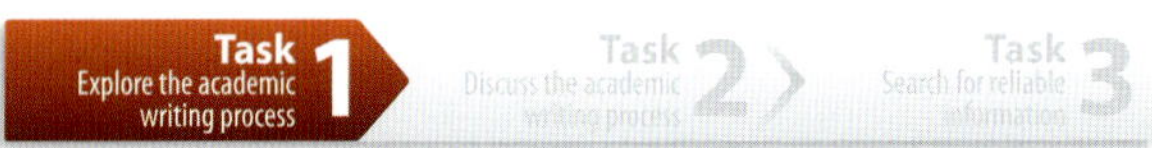

Task 1
Explore the academic writing process

Put the following steps into the correct order. Also, decide the approximate percentage each step would take in the total writing process. Then, compare your answers with those of the person next to you. This should take you five minutes.

- Synthesizing
- Searching for a range of information on the topic from different viewpoints
- Editing
- Reading and selecting relevant information from the sources
- Writing
- Note-taking
- Identifying which of the sources are good academic sources of information

Step	Name of Step	Percentage of total time taken
Step 1		
Step 2		
Step 3		
Step 4		

Step 5

Step 6

Step 7

Academic writing process

Good academic writing does not start with the actual writing. There are many steps you need to go through **before** you start writing. Look at the following description of a typical academic writing process.

Searching for a range of information on the topic from different viewpoints

Identifying which of the sources are good academic sources of information

Reading and selecting relevant information from the sources

Note-taking

Synthesizing

Writing

Editing

Students tend to think that writing should take the longest amount of time, but usually, searching for information, reading and selecting information to refer to in your writing will take the most time. Students also tend to spend far too little time editing their written work.

You will practise all these steps throughout this course.

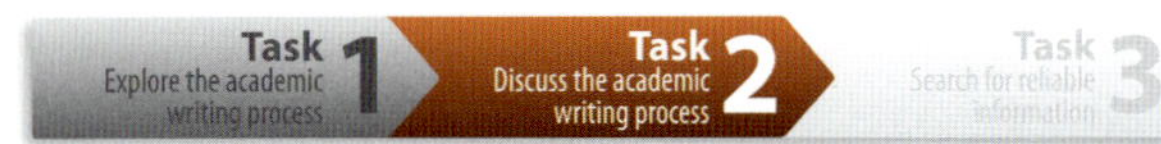

Task 2
Discuss the academic writing process

Think about the type of writing that you did at secondary school. Answer the following questions with your partner. Take ten minutes to do this task.

- Did you follow these steps?
- Which did you do well?
- Which did you find difficult?
- How might writing at university be different from writing at secondary school?

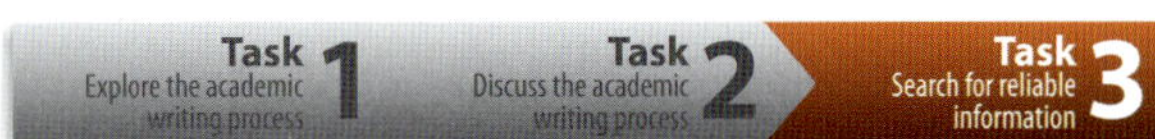

Task 3
Search for reliable information

Your teacher will show you how to search for academic information using Google Scholar and the library electronic databases. Make notes in the box below. It should take you ten minutes to do this.

How to use the library electronic databases

How to use Google Scholar

Homework
Apply skills to another course

Search for three texts that you think are relevant reading for one course that you are taking at the moment. Search for them on Google Scholar and on electronic databases. These texts should not be on a reading list given to you. Once you have found them, copy down the references. In less than 300 words, explain:

- which texts you are going to read
- why you have chosen them and not others
- how easy/difficult it was to find them using Google Scholar and electronic databases
- why you think they are good academic sources of information

Academic Vocabulary

Understanding collocation

What is collocation?

Collocation is putting two or more things together, especially words in a pattern; these words co-occur **more often than expected by chance**. Some examples of common collocations in English: it's raining cats and dogs; commit a crime, not do a crime; strong tea, not powerful tea; but a powerful computer, not a strong computer.

Correct collocations	Incorrect collocations
great <u>fun</u>	*large* fun [lots of fun is also okay; great doesn't refer to size]
make a <u>mistake</u>	*make* a fault [not do a mistake; make an error is okay]
The <u>coat</u> is **torn**.	The coat is *broken*. [soft things tear; hard things break]

Why should I learn collocations?

Learning collocations will help you to **express yourself naturally** in both written and spoken English.

How can I learn collocations?

First of all, you need to be aware of how words go together as you read or listen to others. As you come across new vocabulary, try to learn the expression as a whole. You can familiarize yourself with collocations in natural contexts by reading and listening to English as much as possible.

You can consider keeping a vocabulary log with collocations and examples. Write down the collocates of a particular word (e.g., 'complete': a complete **set**, a complete **list**, a complete **report**, your **work** is complete) by consulting dictionaries or using a concordancer (see below).

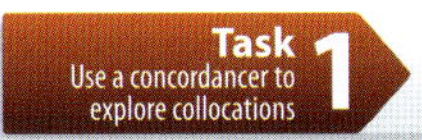

Task 1
Use a concordancer to explore collocations

Collocations can be in the form of combinations of different word classes (e.g., noun + noun, noun + adverb, noun + adjective). Below is a selected list of collocations taken from the articles in the *South China Morning Post* using the *PolyU Web Concordancer*. Highlight the word **complete** and the surrounding words. Then work out the different types of collocations and complete the table. The first one has been done for you as an example. It should take you ten minutes to do this task.

Concordances for *complete* = 87   Net Dictionary entries for complete

1   cing a drug addict to allow him to **complete** a 100-day mourning period for his fa
2   Vu said. {para} He said they would **complete** a petition in the next few days and
3   n Chek Lap Kok and is scheduled to **complete** a West Kowloon Reclamation contract
4   rivate property market, which could **complete** about 35,000 flats a year, he said.
5   the project will take 45 months to **complete** . About six of the 20 hectares of re
6   ra} "We don't see videotaping as a **complete** alternative," he said. {/article}
7   t the central Government has yet to **complete** an investigation into the stock cr
8   ocal administration should table a **complete** and substantial financial package o
9   he new airport construction plan is **complete** , and the financial arrangement is c
10 n in when the Siu Lam extension was **complete** , another 200 would go to the Tuen M
11 sers, to make it as accessible and **complete** as possible. {para} The information
12 to give the two municipal councils **complete** autonomy to decide their fees. {par
13 re Lantau Fixed Crossing is almost **complete** before deciding whether to grant an
14 hnically, it is not so difficult to **complete** , but there are problems with logist
15 introduce the price-capping will be **complete** by the end of the year. {para} Hong
16 } {headline} Star-crossed paths BY **complete** coincidence two chart-toppers of th
17 nson. {para} "But the survey was a **complete** cross-section of the public and did
18 n mid-1993 and take 2 1/2 years to **complete** . Current premises are spread around
19 ture is clearer now, but it is not **complete** enough." {para} Imelda Marcos was
20 ng link in Kowloon and I still have **complete** faith in the project," he said. {p

(Source: the *PolyU Web Concordancer*, http://vlc.polyu.edu.hk/concordance/WWWConcappE.htm)

	Types of collocations	Examples given
1	Verb + Noun	Complete a petition, complete a contract
2		
3		

Task 2
Use a concordancer and dictionaries

Now, with your partner, work out the differences between the following pairs of words by consulting the Collins WordBanksOnline English corpus sampler available at http://www.collins.co.uk/Corpus/CorpusSearch. aspx and any dictionary. Use two examples from the concordancer to illustrate your points. This task should take you fifteen minutes.

(A) everyday versus every day

(B) beside versus besides

(C) principle versus principal

(D) lay versus lie

(E) loose versus lose

Academic Speaking

Task 1
Discuss your experience of academic speaking

The following are some common types of speaking that students have to do at university. Tick the ones you have experience doing in English and in Chinese. Take ten minutes to do this task.

	English	Chinese
Giving a formal presentation using PowerPoint		
Participating in a tutorial discussion		
Leading a tutorial discussion		
Speaking with a teacher one-on-one about a problem or a question		
Discussing feedback on your written work with your teacher		
Discussing your studies with other students outside of class		

Now, discuss the following with your partner.

Which of these activities do you think are easier? Why?

Which of these activities do you think are harder? Why?

What different speaking skills do these activities require?

Task 2
Self-assess your speaking skills

Look at the following speaking skills. Rate their difficulty for you. When you have finished, compare your list with that of your partner. It should take you ten minutes to do this task.

	I can do this well	I can do this fairly well	I need quite a lot of practice
I can speak without making too many grammatical mistakes.			
I can speak without too many hesitations.			
I can usually find the words I need to say what I want.			
My pronunciation is mostly clear.			
I am confident of speaking in front of people.			
I can get my message across in a group discussion.			

When you have finished, compare your answers with those of the person next to you. If you have ticked "I need quite a lot of practice" for anything, discuss what you need to do to improve.

Academic speaking at university

One of the most common types of speaking assignments for university undergraduates is the **tutorial discussion**. Most students have participated in group discussions at secondary school, but the tutorial discussion is a bit different from a secondary school group discussion.

The purpose of a tutorial discussion

Tutorial discussions are supposed to be a learning activity for students. They are a chance for students to discuss key academic concepts, find out if they understand those concepts, discuss the concepts from different points of view and therefore reach a deeper understanding of those concepts than if they were just learning by themselves. Because of this, the more you participate, the more you learn. In order to participate effectively, you need certain discussion skills.

Discussion skills

You need to be able to:

- give your opinion clearly and concisely

- agree and disagree with others' opinions when necessary

- ask for clarification when necessary

- listen to what other students say and add your own opinion

Content

What you say should:

- discuss the complexity of the issues

- give good evidence to support personal opinions

- be referenced to good academic sources of information

- make conclusions which are well-argued and logical

Task 1
Prepare for tutorial discussion

You have fifteen minutes to prepare for your first tutorial discussion. Get into groups of four. Each student in the group should choose a different text on pages 33–36. Read your text. Make notes below in point form, both from the article and your own knowledge.

For this tutorial, you should focus on:

- giving evidence to support your personal opinions

- expressing your opinion in a well-argued and logical manner

- acknowledging and discussing the complexities of the topic

	Opinion	Evidence
How serious is the childhood obesity problem around the world?		
What are the causes of this problem?		
What do you think the solutions are?		

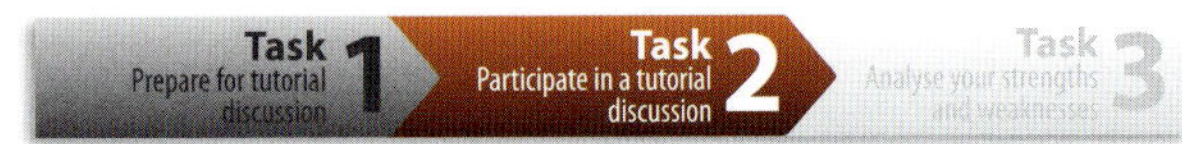

Task 2

Participate in a tutorial discussion

Now, hold a tutorial discussion for thirty minutes. Remember to:

1. use ideas and data from the text to support your opinions

2. change written language from the texts into spoken language

3. speak naturally rather than read directly from the text

4. use citation vocabulary when necessary to strengthen the evidence you use to support your opinions

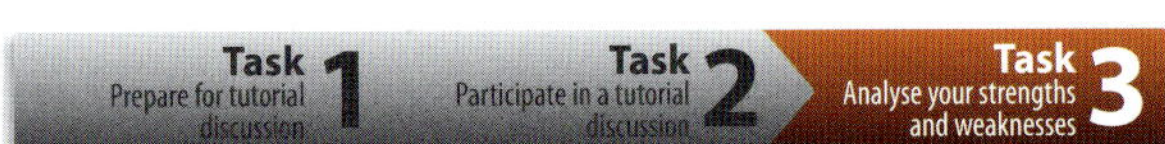

Task 3

Analyse your strengths and weaknesses

Take five minutes to fill in the Tutorial Discussion Feedback form.

Tutorial Discussion Feedback Form			
My ideas were clearly expressed.	☐ Yes	☐ No	☐ Sometimes
I was able to express myself without frequent hesitations.	☐ Yes	☐ No	☐ Sometimes
I know enough vocabulary to be able to express my thoughts and opinions.	☐ Yes	☐ No	☐ Sometimes
I integrated the information from my reading into the discussion to support my arguments.	☐ Yes	☐ No	☐ Sometimes
I expressed my agreement with others' ideas.	☐ Yes	☐ No	☐ Sometimes
I expressed my disagreement with others' ideas when necessary and gave reasons.	☐ Yes	☐ No	☐ Sometimes
I helped develop some kind of agreement/consensus when possible.	☐ Yes	☐ No	☐ Sometimes
I helped maintain good group relations by being polite, listening to others and not interrupting.	☐ Yes	☐ No	☐ Sometimes

Ideas for future improvement

Text 1

Child obesity 'cause for concern'

West Australian researchers say the child obesity epidemic is real, and a new study shows nearly one in three 14-year-olds is at risk of future heart disease.

The University of West Australia study, which tracked some 3,000 children from birth, aims to challenge suggestions the 'obesity epidemic' is not real.

The findings, to be published in the July *Medical Journal of Australia Today*, showed 29% of 14-year-olds were at high risk of cardiovascular disease. And one in four children aged eight were also at increased risk.

Dr Rae-Chi Huang said the study showed childhood obesity was a real threat.

Heart Foundation chief executive Lynn Roberts suggested the proportion of obese or overweight 7- to 15-year-olds had doubled between 1985 and 2011.

"This trend is a cause for concern, given the widely recognized body of evidence on the significant short-term and long-term consequences of heart disease," Dr Roberts said.

Compiling data from three national surveys, the researchers from the Heart Foundation and the International Association for the Study of Obesity found 24% of boys in the 7- to 15-year-old age bracket were overweight or obese in 2007. For girls the proportion was 26%.

In January, a study from the University of South Australia suggested obesity rates among children stopped increasing around 1998 and have since remained steady. But Heart Foundation spokesman Maurice Swanson said the two latest reports emphatically showed the reality of childhood obesity.

"What these two studies confirm is that there is an epidemic of overweight and obesity in Australia," he said. "It's not a myth."

Dr Huang said the children at risk often were born to mothers who smoked while pregnant, or to overweight or obese mothers.

Children not breastfed or breastfed for too short a time also appeared to be more at risk.

"It's really a wake-up call that we can't be complacent about it," Dr Huang said. "We really need to act now, and not wait until these children reach adulthood."

Canberra Daily, Australia

Text 2

Childhood obesity stops increasing; but a third still at risky weight

Finally some good news in the weight-loss struggle: The rate of childhood obesity may have stopped increasing in the USA after years of rapid growth, new government data show.

About 31% of children and teens ages 2 to 19 — about 23 million — were either overweight or obese in 2003–06 compared with 29% in 1999. The increase is not considered statistically significant.

There also was no statistically significant increase in the percentage of children who are the heaviest. About 16% of kids ages 2 and older were obese in 2003–11, compared with 14% in 1999–2000. But the percentage is still far higher than the 5% to 7% of children who were obese in 1980.

"It looks like childhood obesity has stopped increasing after 20 years of growth," says lead researcher Cynthia Ogden, an epidemiologist with the National Center for Health Statistics, part of the Center for Disease Control and Prevention. "We can be cautiously optimistic that things are beginning to stabilize, but these percentages are still higher than they should be."

Experts have known for years that carrying extra weight is problematic for children's health. It puts them at an increased risk for Type 2 diabetes, high cholesterol, and other health problems. "This shows some hope that the message is finally getting through," says David Ludwig, director of the Optimal Weight for Life Program at Children's Hospital in Boston. "However, no matter what, the current levels are still unacceptably high."

The latest statistics are based on measurements of 8,165 children and adolescents who were part of the National Health and Nutrition Examination Survey in 2003 to 2011. Most experts classify children as obese if their BMI is larger than that of 95% of the total population.

Children are considered overweight if they fall between the 85th and 95th percentile on the BMI (Body Mass Index) growth charts. Ludwig, author of an accompanying editorial in the journal, believes a comprehensive national campaign is needed to attack childhood obesity, including legislation to protect children "from junk-food advertising."

In the meantime, parents must keep highly processed foods out of the house, limit time spent at the TV and computer and set a good example with their own exercise and eating habits, he says.

USA Times, The USA

Text 3

One teenager's struggle with weight

SHANGHAI: For the past decade, Huang Qing has seen her waistline get bigger at a frightening rate. "My waistline has already grown past the tape measure," said the 17-year-old in Shanghai, whose weight has increased from 140 kg to 210 kg in the past four years, four to five times the weight of most people her age.

Wearing a loose red T-shirt and black sweatpants, Huang moves very slowly about in her home. "To be frank, I even find it difficult to get up from the bed," she said.

Huang's weight has increased so much that she has broken four chairs at home. To avoid this, the girl has to spend the majority of the day lying on her bed. She also quit school two years ago and is unwilling to walk outside her home — both for fear of being laughed at and because of a lack of energy, said her mother, Jin Ming.

"No one is sure how she got like this as she does not eat that much, but after the age of 6 her weight just kept on increasing without obvious reason," Jin said. In the family battle against the bulge, Jin said they had tried every means possible to help Huang lose weight, including acupuncture, diet pills, swimming and judo. But nothing worked.

While youth such as Huang may be an extreme case of childhood obesity, its occurrence among adolescents is on the rise in the country. One possible factor is that food availability has increased as people are richer. Children are also not doing enough exercise, especially in cities. National surveys on the health of schoolchildren showed that the obesity among children between 7 and 18 had increased four times from 1985 to 2010. And figures for the number of overweight children in the same age range and time period had increased 28 times. This increase parallels the increasing availability of cheap, calorie-laden fast food.

It is difficult to know how to help severely overweight children like Huang Qing. It seems that, once weight increases to such a level, half the battle is psychological. Severely overweight children often suffer from an extreme lack of self-esteem and are often clinically depressed. Research conducted by Dr Leung in the Faculty of Medicine at Washington University has shown that the incidence of depression among obese children might be as high as 96%. He recommends that parents try to help their children build up their self-esteem and help them to establish a healthy lifestyle as much as possible. "Parents and society need to understand that it is more important to help children develop a healthy lifestyle than stop them eating. If they can do this, weight loss should follow. All children have a right to be happy and healthy."

The China Post, China

Text 4

Super size Hong Kong

Grandparents, junk food and too much homework may be the reason for Hong Kong's rising obesity problem. According to a study by the Sports Science Department at the University of Hong Kong, 16.8% of girls and 22.5% of boys were overweight in 2010, compared with only 8.9% and 11.3% in 2000. Professor Li, who runs a clinic for obese children with the Sports Science Department, says caregivers and schools play very important roles in children's attitudes towards life.

"Parents are role models. If they don't exercise or they eat a lot of junk food, their children will copy their behaviour," he says. Regina Lee, assistant professor of nursing at Hong Kong Polytechnic University, agrees. "Parents are busy working nowadays, so both adults and children have become less active. Children do little exercise and have bad eating habits because they learn from their parents." Dr Lee says parents who have obese children mistakenly believe the children have inherited bad genes.

In the past, fast-food chains were relatively expensive and fast food was seen as occasional treats. Now, prices have dropped and the number of outlets has increased. This means children have easy access to unhealthy snacks, Dr Lee says. When both parents work, fast food is seen as an easy alternative to home-cooked meals.

Parents are not the only caregivers for many Hong Kong children, however. Albert Li Man-chim, of the Chinese University of Hong Kong, says: "Many children are looked after by their grandparents, who still think being fat is cute and healthy and brings good luck. They allow their grandchildren to eat whatever they want."

Children are also spending more time studying, watching TV and using the computer than going out to play, says Daphne Wu, a dietician at Matilda International Hospital. "Some parents prefer their children to study or take extra classes rather than exercise in their spare time. After studying, children watch TV or go online. There's not much physical activity," says Ms Wu.

Stanley Hui Sai-chuen, Associate Professor in the Sports Science Department at the University of Hong Kong, said it was easy for Hong Kong children to get hold of high-calorie foods, but they did not offset the effects of these foods by exercising. "Children do not even have to walk much or climb stairs nowadays, which reduces their chance of burning calories," he said at the International Conference on Childhood Obesity. "This has all led to the current obesity problem that we now face in Hong Kong."

Hong Kong News, Hong Kong

Gathering information for your assignments

Test your knowledge

Answer these questions about Unit 2 with your partner.

1. When you are given a written assignment, what do you need to do before you start writing?

2. How should you take notes while reading texts for a writing assignment?

3. How do you prepare yourself for a speaking tutorial?

4. How is spoken language different from written language?

Learning outcomes

By the end of this unit, you should be able to:

- use textual features for fast reading and note-taking;

- analyse writing assignment titles;

- use linking words and phrases to improve coherence in writing;

- gather ideas or data for your writing;

- take notes and paraphrase ideas or data from sources;

- transform written language into spoken language when preparing for a tutorial discussion; and

- use vocabulary for referring to sources of information in a tutorial discussion.

Overview of Unit

One of the biggest differences between secondary school and university is the **amount of reading** you are expected to do. You are also expected to read very different types of text as well, ones with more complex concepts in them. In order to complete the written and spoken assignments for your courses, you will be expected to do a lot of reading so you can **understand the assignment topic in depth**. Reading will give you information to support the arguments you wish to make in your writing and speaking.

In Unit 1, you were shown how to use library electronic databases and Google Scholar to identify good academic sources of information for academic writing and speaking assignments. You were also shown some of the typical characteristics of good academic writing and speaking at university. In Unit 2 you will start to practise academic writing and speaking skills by learning how to gather and record information for your writing and speaking assignments.

Preparing to gather information by analysing assignment topics

It is important for you to be able to **focus your reading** on your specific assignment topic.

To do this, you have to understand the requirements of that assignment. You will need to ask yourself:

- What does the assignment title or question mean?
- What kind of information do I need to look for in my reading?

Task 1
Choose an assignment topic

Look at the following assignment topics. Think about which one you would choose. Tell the person next to you which one you would choose and why. Take ten minutes to do this.

Essay Topic

Write an essay comparing and contrasting the concepts of fair trade and free trade. Highlight the benefits and dangers for developing countries.

Report Topic

Write a report investigating the perceptions of Hong Kong citizens of fair-trade products, and analyse the feasibility of setting up a fair-trade shop in Central.

Tutorial Discussion Topic

Is globalization a positive influence in developing countries in Asia, or a negative one?

Analysis of assignment topics

The first step in completing a writing assignment is to **analyse the topic** you have been given. You will then be able to **focus** your reading **efficiently**. Here is a six-step process you can go through to do this.

Step One: Circle the **directive verbs**, if there are any, e.g. *compare and contrast*. Think about what they are asking you to do.

Step Two: Underline the **main content words**. Think about what they mean.

Step Three: Think about **what kind of information you will need to read** in order to complete the assignment.

Step Four: Write **a basic outline/plan** for the assignment.

Step Five: Use the outline/plan to **make headings for your note-taking**.

Step Six: Think about **what kinds of text** would have the information you are looking for that are **also good sources of academic information**.

Task 2
Analyse assignment topics

Look at the example of the analysis of an essay topic. Fill in the gaps for the analysis of the report topic. Compare your answers with those of your partner. Take fifteen minutes to do this.

Steps	Analysis of essay topic	Analysis of report topic
1. Circle the directive verbs, if there are any. Think about what they are asking you to do.	*Write an essay* ==comparing== *and* ==contrasting== *the concepts of fair trade and free trade.* ==Highlight== *the benefits and dangers for developing countries.* • *Compare and contrast is asking you to find similarities and differences.* • *Highlight is asking you to give special emphasis to something.* You can see that there are two parts to the essay. This should give you an idea about how to organize it.	*Write a report* ==investigating== *the perceptions of Hong Kong citizens of fair-trade products, and* ==analyse== *the feasibility of setting up a fair-trade shop in Central.* • *Investigate is asking you to* ___________ . • *Analyse is asking you to* ___________ .

2. Underline the main content words. Think about what they mean.	*Write an essay comparing and contrasting the concepts of <u>fair trade</u> and <u>free trade</u>. Highlight the <u>benefits</u> and <u>dangers</u> for <u>developing countries</u>.* Key terms like these are often complicated and have several definitions, depending on your political, economic, and ethical stance. Try to find different definitions and compare them. It is important to find definitions for the following terms: • fair trade • free trade • developing countries	*Write a report investigating the <u>perceptions of Hong Kong citizens</u> of <u>fair-trade products</u>, and analyse the <u>feasibility</u> of setting up a <u>fair-trade shop</u> in <u>Central</u>.* Think about what the above underlined words mean before you start reading about the topic:
3. Think about what kind of information you will need to find in order to complete the assignment.	By underlining the key words and the directive verbs, you can see that there are points of comparison. You need to find: • differences and similarities in free trade and fair trade • examples of the benefits and dangers of both concepts	You need to find:
4. Write an outline for the essay.	This is a very important step. An outline will give you a clearer idea of what you need to read. Here is an example of one possible outline: Paragraph 1 Introduction • Definitions of fair trade and free trade • Definition of developing countries Paragraph 2 • Differences and similarities in fair trade and free trade Paragraph 3 • Benefits and dangers of fair trade Paragraph 4 • Benefits and dangers of free trade Paragraph 5 • Your point of view about which has the most benefits/dangers overall Paragraph 6 Conclusion • Summary and look to the future	Here is an example of one possible outline: 1. Summary 2. Introduction 3. 4. 5. 6. 7. 8. 9. Conclusion

| 5. Use the outline to make headings for your note-taking. | Here are the most logical headings to use for note-taking:

1. Definition of fair trade
2. Definition of free trade
3. Definition of developing countries
4. Examples of benefits of fair trade
5. Examples of dangers of fair trade
6. Examples of benefits of free trade
7. Examples of dangers of free trade | The following headings cover all the information that has to be collected on the topic:

1. Perceptions

1.1 List of fair-trade products for sale in Hong Kong

1.2 Perceptions of Hong Kong citizens of these products

2. Feasibility study

2.1 Estimation of costs of running a small shop in different parts of Central, by looking at rental costs, utilities, employment costs, taxation, etc.

2.2 Estimation of turnover needed to make a profit |
| **6. Think about what kind of texts would have the information you are looking for.** | This kind of information is likely to be found in:

• books on fair trade/free trade
• journal articles in journals related to business/politics/trade
• websites of NGOs
• websites from the WTO, UN etc. | This kind of information is likely to be found in:

• |

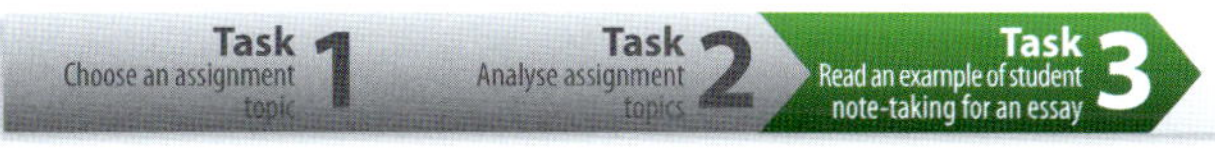

Task 3
Read an example of student note-taking for an essay

Match the student's notes with the right heading. Write the correct number in the blank column. Compare your answers with those of your partner. Take five minutes to do this.

Outline	Student's notes
I. **Definitions of free trade**	• better incomes for growers; growers sell their produce at a higher price when number of intermediaries is reduced, e.g. cocoa farmers in Ghana (Gregory 2010) • improved health care and infrastructure: part of the higher incomes earned by the growers is invested in a community fund to provide capital for improving medical care and infrastructure (Gardner 2008) • environmental protection: regulations set up to ensure manufacturers observe national & international laws concerning waste management & protection of natural resources, e.g. water & forests (World Fair Trade Organization 2010) • better working conditions: regulations set up to monitor working hours & safety, no forced labour allowed, use of child labour must be disclosed & monitored (WFTO 2010)

2. **Definitions of fair trade**		• the World Bank categorizes countries according to income per capita: classifies all low- and middle-income countries as developing countries
		• the UN includes life expectancy & literacy rates in its classification: developing countries have a low level of industrialization & low standard of living (UN 2008)
		• e.g. of countries: mostly in Africa & Latin America (UN 2008)
3. **Definitions of developing countries**		• "Free trade is the ability to sell your goods without unnecessary regulation, e.g. sales tax" (Smith 2001: 35)
		• does not focus on ethical considerations; it lets the market work out the price of goods (Jones 1999)
4. **Benefits of fair trade**		• foreign investment led to economic growth (e.g. China and India), increased incomes for some citizens in some parts of the country (World Bank 2005)
		• lower prices of imported & exported goods due to removal of tariffs (WTO 2008)
5. **Dangers of fair trade**		• international companies look for cheapest labour & raw materials → reduced wages & poor working conditions for growers and factory workers, e.g. Uganda & El Salvador (Houston 2010)
		• wider income disparity: unequal distribution of wealth/income brought by opening of economy, e.g. China (Chan 2004) & India (Jha 2005)
6. **Benefits of free trade**		• "Fair trade focuses on the ethics surrounding the production of goods including giving growers a fair price for their products and ensuring no exploitation of children or low-paid workers." (Chan 2003: 12)
		• "Fair trade is seen by some as anything but fair. It leads to unnecessary restrictions and too much artificial control of the marketing process." (Winter 2005: 4)
7. **Dangers of free trade**		• international companies use "fair trade" label as a mask to expand corporate interest in developing countries: control information to favour their business, e.g. sugar plantation workers in Asia still work in poor conditions and receive low pay (Hale 2008)
		• growers (e.g. nut growers in Brazil) working for international companies become more dependent on them and less self-reliant (Graham 2009)
		• local governments reduce funding for education, health, environmental protection etc., thinking these are projects are funded by fair-trade partners (Fisher 2009)

Task 4
Analyse a topic on your own

Now carry out your own analysis on the tutorial discussion topic. It should take you fifteen minutes to do this. Do it with the person sitting next to you.

Is globalization a positive influence in developing countries in Asia, or a negative one?

Steps	Analysis
1. Circle the directive verbs, if there are any. Think about what they are asking you to do.	Is globalization a positive influence in developing countries in Asia, or a negative one?
2. Underline the main content words. Think about what they mean.	Is globalization a positive influence in developing countries in Asia, or a negative one?
3. Think about what kind of information you will need to participate in the discussion in order to support your point of view.	
5. Make the points into headings for your note-taking.	
6. Think about what kinds of text would have the information you are looking for.	Is globalization a positive influence in developing countries in Asia, or a negative one?

Academic Reading

Gathering information using textual signals

The six steps discussed above will help you to **prepare to read**. Once you have done this and you have headings for your note-taking, you need to read and take notes.

Task 1
Give your opinions on globalization

Globalization means an increase in free trade and open markets throughout the world, usually accompanied by an increase in the international dominance of multinational corporations; or more simply, it's the trend towards an integrated global economy. Before you read an article about globalization, discuss in a small group for five minutes whether you think the following phenomena related to globalization are good or bad.

1. Globalized media such as satellite TV, imported magazines, and the Internet

2. Free trade increasing the import and export of goods across nations

3. Cheaper and more efficient transport

4. Corporations moving production and operations to developing countries to reduce labour costs

5. Increasing use of English and decreasing variation in local dialects

Using textual signals for quick reading and note-taking

You will not have time to read every text in depth when you are completing an assignment for your courses. You need to start by **skimming and scanning** by using the **headings for your note-taking** to see whether there is information relevant to your assignment. After that, you can go back and read more closely the sections that are relevant, if you need to. The following are some suggested strategies to help you do your first reading efficiently.

Reading for the main idea of the text

The main idea or argument that the writer wants to present in a journal article or book chapter is often given **near the end of an introductory paragraph** or in an **abstract**. This statement captures the main idea or argument of the text. It is very important that you understand the overall argument/position of the writer, whether he or she agrees/disagrees/partially agrees with the issues discussed; otherwise, it is unlikely that you will understand the details. The main argument is usually restated in the concluding paragraph as well. This is not always the case for other texts that you might be reading for your other courses. For example, news texts do not always have a clear main argument from the writer because news is supposed to be objective. You can often find opinions in the text, as well as bias, but if they are there they tend to be spread throughout the text and are less obvious.

Reading for the main idea of the paragraph

The beginning sentence of each body paragraph usually announces the topic of that paragraph and is often called a topic sentence. Reading these beginning sentences of the body paragraphs can help you obtain a quick understanding of the main points explored in the article. Sometimes, **the ending sentence of a paragraph** summarizes what is in the paragraph, and therefore it may be useful to look at the ending of each paragraph as well. Again, not all texts have clear topic sentences. Each paragraph in any text should have a focused topic of some kind, however.

Reading for the structure of the text

Linking words or phrases such as 'one of the … is', 'another … is', 'moreover', 'although …', 'however' are used in texts to indicate the relationships between ideas, e.g. the next idea being an addition to the previous one, a result, a contrasting idea, etc. These linking words or phrases are **often used at the beginning of paragraphs to indicate the transition between two paragraphs**. By understanding the use of these words or phrases in a text, you can understand the structure of the arguments presented in the text.

Task 2
Discuss globalization

Imagine that you are writing an essay on the following topic:

> Jimmy Carter, the 39th president of the US, once said, "Globalization, as defined by rich people like us, is a very nice thing; you are talking about the Internet, you are talking about cell phones, you are talking about computers. However, this doesn't affect two-thirds of the people of the world." **Do you agree with this statement? Discuss the effects of globalization on developing countries in the 21st century.**

Take five minutes to tell your partner whether you agree or disagree with the statement made by Jimmy Carter. Explain why.

Task 3
Use textual signals for quick reading and note-taking

Now, read part of a book chapter (some of the text has been taken out) on this topic, and make some notes for this essay. Using what you have learnt so far about quick reading, fill in the note-taking table. You have only five minutes to do this.

The author's main argument	Advantages of globalization	Disadvantages of globalization
Examples of how globalization is affecting different countries	China: India:	Ecuador: El Salvador: Uganda:

CHAPTER 3

Has globalization improved living standards in the developing world?

Angela Hudson

Globalization leads to countries being more connected and interdependent culturally, economically and politically. Economically, it has led to an enormous increase in international trade and investment across different countries, resulting in an increase in wealth and living standards for many countries. For example, the average yearly income per person in China rose from US$1,460 in 1980 to US$4,120 in 1999 ("Change of China's GDP" 2008). However, the gap between the richest and the poorest around the world has increased from 30 to 1 in 1960 to 82 to 1 in 1995 (Purdue 2004). Not all countries, or people within those countries, benefit from globalization equally. In many developing countries, Western companies are maximizing profits by using cheap labour and raw materials ("Africa: Stand up" 2008). Often, globalization benefits the Western companies, not the people in developing countries. While globalization does benefit some people, it does not, on the whole, improve living standards in developing countries, specifically countries in Africa and Latin America. This can be seen through lower wages, falling literacy rates and life expectancy.

One of the many benefits of globalization lies in the form of foreign direct investment (FDI), which has greatly influenced the economies of developing countries. In the past few decades, many Western companies have started to buy raw materials from developing countries and have moved their factories to these places to reduce labour costs. Such foreign investment plays a key role in technology transfer, in industrial restructuring, and the setup of transnational organizations. This has led to greater wealth for some people in these developing economies, especially in China and India. For instance, China has had an average annual GDP growth of 8% over the past 25 years ("Change of China's GDP" 2008) because of its export of goods to America. Similarly, India has enjoyed an annual 6% economic growth since it opened up its economy in the 1990s (Wong 2009). In both countries, economic growth has reduced the number of citizens living in extreme poverty, although this has not been spread evenly across the country. This is especially so in the case of China, as the wealth tends to be concentrated in areas along the coast.

There are many other examples of the advantages of globalization. [text taken out]

However, what seems like an advantage is sometimes a hidden disadvantage. [text taken out]

Although globalization is benefiting developing countries such as China and India, it has not improved the living standards of many of the citizens in Africa and Latin America. The demand for cheap labour and raw materials means that international companies keep moving their production and raw materials bases to ever cheaper places. As a result, developing countries are competing with each other to offer the cheapest possible products. This often leads to lower wages and even poorer working conditions than previously. For example, in an international clothing magazine, an advertisement in 1990 read "You can hire a clothing factory worker for 57 cents a year in El Salvador". One year later, the salary was halved to 33 cents in the same advertisement (Asner et al. 2000).

Another example is coffee growers in Uganda, Africa. They have to sell their coffee beans to intermediaries at prices so low that they cannot even cover their own production costs. Many of their children are forced to leave school, and the family are left without money to buy food. These farmers cannot raise prices because corporations would just buy coffee beans from even cheaper sources such as Vietnam (Metcalf 2007). Banana growers in Ecuador are also paid poorly by intermediaries, while a few international companies that dominate the banana trade make huge profits from selling the fruit (Morris 2003). These workers and their families in developing economies suffer from poor working and living conditions.

Moreover, economic growth caused by foreign investment does not necessarily mean improvement in the living standards of the citizens. Living standards are reflected in the life expectancy and literacy rates of the citizens. In most of Africa and Latin America, children have to work on farms and are denied access to education; healthcare is inadequate and life expectancies are lower than other developed nations (Dannaher 2003). Also, over the past two decades, the poverty rates have increased in Africa by 33% (Lerman 2002). Globalization in developing economies has not improved the quality of living of the citizens.

It is a complicated issue to decide how to ensure that developing countries have access to employment opportunities but at the same time are not exploited. [text taken out]

It seems that globalization has helped international companies make larger profits but failed to raise the living standards of many people living in poverty, especially those in Africa and Latin America, because of the competition for cheap labour and raw materials. Regulation is needed to protect the wages and working conditions of workers in these developing economies.

References

Africa: Stand up, be counted. (2008, July 31). *Africa News*, p. 5.

Asner, E., J. Brecher, T. Costello, & B. Smith. (2000). *Global village or global pillage?* [S.I.]: Stone Soup.

Change of China's GDP Over 20 Years. (2008, December 21). *CRIEnglish.com*. Retrieved 21 December 2008, from http://english.cri.cn/855/2005/09/03/192@16626.htm.

Dannaher, B. (2003). *Impacts of globalization*. Warriewood, NSW: Classroom Video.

Lee, H. W. (2007, May 1). Concept of fair trade still novel to locals. *Korean Times*, p. 1.

Lerman, R. I. (2002). *Globalization and the fight against poverty*. Retrieved 21 December 2008, from http://www.urban.org/publications/410612.html.

Metcalf, F. (2007, September 1). Inequality difficult to digest. *The Courier Mail (Austraila)*, p. M18.

Morris, S. (2003, May 17). Food: Why we eat this way: Unfair trade winds: What do Ecuadorean bananas, Ugandan coffee and English apples, have in common? No power. *The Guardian*, p. 26. Retrieved 23 December 2008, from International Newsstand database.

Purdue, K. (2004). *Globalization: Winner and losers*. Princeton, NJ: Films for the Humanities & Sciences.

Wong, J. (2009). *Asian economy*. Hong Kong: Hong Kong University Press.

Apply skills to another course

Write an analysis of one text you have read recently for one of your other courses. It should be an academic text, such as a journal article or a chapter from a book. Use the following questions to guide you. Write up the analysis of the text in less than 300 words. Decide:

1. what the author's main argument is and whether you agree with it

2. whether the text has identifiable topic sentences (give some examples)

3. whether the text has a concluding paragraph, and if it does, whether you think it is a good summary of the whole text

4. what examples of words used in the text show the structure of the text

5. how this text could relate to an assignment that you need to write for your course

Academic Grammar

Comparing and contrasting ideas gathered from reading

Linking words and phrases are used to help a writer to establish clear relationships between ideas within or between paragraphs. They are often used when we point out differences and similarities in ideas, and when pointing out cause-effect relationships.

Noticing how they are used in a text can help you understand the structure of the text more easily. You will also need to use them in your own writing when you are talking about complex academic concepts.

Linking words and phrases can be grouped according to their function (e.g. to introduce an additional idea or a contrasting idea) and grammatical feature.

Task 1
Identify linking words that compare or contrast ideas

Read through the following paragraph. Underline words or phrases that are used to compare or contrast ideas. The first one has been done as an example. This should take you five minutes.

International trade has led to greater wealth for some people in some developing countries. For instance, the overall poverty rate in China fell from 53% in 1981 to 2.5% in 2005 (Han 2008), whereas in India, poverty has declined overall from over 40% in 1985 to below 25% in 2002 (Jha 2006). In both countries, economic growth has reduced the number of citizens living in extreme poverty, although this has not been spread evenly across the country. This is especially so in the case of China, as the wealth tends to concentrate in areas along the east coast. According to some government statistics, the GDP per capita in China's midwest was only 47% of that of the east coast in 2000 (Wang 2002), and 10.8% of people still lived on less than $1 a day in 2006 (Han 2008). India has experienced a rise in regional inequality as well, especially since 1999, when it increased the pace of its market liberalization despite an average GDP growth of over 5.5% per year.

Task 2
Compare and contrast ideas and data

Spend five minutes looking at the sentences below. Decide whether they describe:

- contrasting ideas or data
- similar ideas or data

1. __________________ globalization has increased the wealth and living standards of people in many countries, it has not benefited all countries, or the people within those countries, equally.

2. China has had an 8% annual GDP growth over the past 25 years ("Change of China's GDP" 2008), __________________ countries in Latin America and Africa have not had significant economic growth by globalizing their economies (Lerman 2002).

3. China has had an average annual GDP growth of 8% over the past 25 years ("Change of China's GDP" 2008) because of its export of goods to America. _______________ , India has enjoyed an annual 8% economic growth since it opened its economy in the 1990s (Wong 2009).

4. _______________ the income level of people living in urban areas along the coast, the income level of people living in rural areas is extremely low.

5. International companies are enjoying huge profits by using the cheap labour and raw materials in Third World countries. _______________ , the workers in these Third World countries suffer from poor working and living conditions.

6. __________________ a long tradition of drinking tea, the demand for coffee has been increasing rapidly in China in recent years.

Now decide on an appropriate word or phrase to put in the gap. It should take you ten minutes to do this.

Task 3

Group linking words and phrases

Put the linking words and phrases in the appropriate category in the table below. In each category, add at last one that you know. Take ten minutes to complete this task.

on the contrary	because of	for instance	owing to	while
on the other hand	even though	as well as	as a result	in spite of
consequently	thus	in addition	similarly	also
because of this	nevertheless	whereas	in contrast	conversely
due to	in comparison	compared to		

Similar ideas	Furthermore,
Contrasting ideas	Although …
Cause and effect	Since …
Examples	For example,

Task 4

Improve coherence in writing

Work with a partner for ten minutes and improve the coherence of the following paragraph. Use linking words or phrases listed in the table in Task 3, or others that you know. Don't just add a few words. Rewrite the whole paragraph to make it more coherent.

The majority population in Hong Kong is Chinese. Chinese is the main written language in Hong Kong. Cantonese is the main spoken language. Ever since Hong Kong became a British colony, English has been the official language and is the main language used in the government. English has become important in the business world and schools. It is not used in everyday life for most people. English is taught in schools. English is used by employees who work in foreign companies. English is not used in a lot of local companies. Putonghua has gained importance since the 1997 handover. English remains one of the two official languages in Hong Kong. English continues to enjoy a high status in most people's minds. People like to add English words into a sentence or mix English and Chinese when people communicate, either verbally or in writing.

Revised paragraph

Homework

Compare and contrast ideas and data from different sources

Imagine you are writing an essay with the following title:

Describe the rising influence of American culture in China. Is it a threat?

Write a paragraph comparing and contrasting the ideas and data taken from these three excerpts in no more than 200 words. Use the note-taking and paraphrasing skills you have learnt. Also use linking words and phrases for comparison and contrast where appropriate.

Excerpt 1

An excerpt of an article written by Celine Sun, entitled "Coffee revolution arrives in China", published in the *China Daily* on 29 November 2010, p. 8

Despite a long tradition of drinking tea, China's thirst for coffee is surging. According to the China Coffee Association in Beijing, consumption of instant coffee has grown 30% annually in recent years. Last year, Chinese people drank nearly 75,000 tons of coffee, compared with 150,000 tons of tea. Although tea is still the most popular beverage, consumption of coffee is predicted to surpass consumption of tea within three decades.

Coffee was introduced into modern China by Swiss-based coffee maker Nestlé in the 1980s. For many years, it was seen by most Chinese as a high-class gift for friends rather than the daily beverage of personal choice. "There were cases in which people who did not like coffee threw out the coffee but kept the jars to drink tea out of," said Ji Ning, president of the Beijing-based Coffee Association.

In the 1990s, coffee shops started to emerge in big cities, playing an important role in promoting a coffee culture and appealing especially to white-collar workers and expatriates. In the last decade, the circle of coffee lovers has been expanding to embrace the new middle class as well as a much younger group of people born in the '80s and '90s. Coffee shops have given these young people a place to meet and socialize. Culturally, this is drawing teenagers out of the home, which used to be their main source of entertainment, and into a social scene which is very much generation-based. Some see this as a threat to traditional Chinese culture, while others see it as a liberating force for the youth of China.

Ji said instant coffee will, in time, become the dominant product in the China market. The average Chinese person currently consumes an average of four cups of coffee weekly but more than twenty cups of tea. The growth potential for coffee in China is huge. Eyeing that vast market, foreign and local companies are bidding against one another for a bigger share of the developing pie.

Starbucks said earlier this year that China will become the second-biggest market behind the US for the company, and they plan to increase the number of mainland stores from 400 to 1,000 in coming years. Hong Kong-based China Resources has also rolled out a plan to open 1,000 more outlets in the country. Fast-food operator McDonald's announced it would add McCafés to 90% of existing restaurants in the country. And Swiss-based food giant Nestlé plans to increase production lines by 75% at its roasting plant in Dongguan, to offer more products domestically.

Excerpt 2

An excerpt of an article written by Julie Jargon, entitled "Starbucks to triple its store count in China", published in the *Wall Street Journal (Online)* on 1 December 2010

Starbucks Corp. plans to more than triple the number of stores it has in mainland China in the next five years, the company said on Wednesday. Starbucks plans to make China its largest market outside the US. The Seattle-based coffee chain currently has 406 stores in China and plans to have more than 1,500 by 2015, the company said at an investor conference in New York.

The company, which has recently enjoyed a turnaround in the US, is trying to focus on expanding its international business, and plans to open 400 new stores around the world next year. Starbucks will continue rolling out its VIVA instant coffee, customizable frappuccino drinks and Starbucks rewards cards, focusing heavily on China, Starbucks International President John Culver told investors.

Mr Culver said the chain plans to expand its 53 international markets more deeply, with an emphasis on China, where store operating profits are higher than they are in the US.

Excerpt 3

An excerpt of an article written by Clifford Coonan, entitled "Starbucks shuts Forbidden City coffee shop", published in the *Irish Times* on 16 July 2007, p. 11

A controversial Starbucks coffee shop in the Forbidden City, the ancient imperial palace in Beijing, closed its doors after two years of opposition. The café was closed last week. It is being turned into a souvenir shop.

The coffee shop was built in the ancient palace, the former residence of the Ming and Qing emperors (14th–20th centuries). When it opened in 2000, it prompted a media backlash so severe that the museum authorities considered revoking its lease after a couple of months.

Last year, a Chinese TV anchorman, Rui Chenggang, began a crusade against the café, saying the US chain's presence in one of the key symbols of the Chinese nation was undermining Chinese culture and marred the solemnity of the Forbidden City. He waged a campaign on his blog and many called for Starbucks to leave the site.

The rectangular palace complex covers 183 acres and is Beijing's top tourist attraction, and had 8.76 million visitors last year. It was listed by Unesco as a World Heritage Site in 1987. There are many stalls selling souvenirs, drinks and other items within the outer courtyards. The site management told the Xinhua News Agency, "We found through a survey that most visitors — from China and abroad — hope to taste some local food rather than coffee from the US".

Academic Writing

Note-taking and paraphrasing

You have already learnt the importance of taking notes under useful headings. However, there are different ways of taking notes. You can write notes in **different formats** such as:

- an outline
- a table
- a mind map

When you write down the ideas of others under your headings, you also need to **avoid plagiarism** by either:

- writing down direct quotes or
- paraphrasing the ideas into your own words

Task 1
Analyse note-taking format

Look at the following notes from a student. Identify the techniques the student has used to take notes in a time-efficient way. It should take you five minutes to do this.

Examples of how globalization is affecting different countries	China: ∴ ↑ foreign investment ↑ Annual GDP, i.e. 8% over 25 years Income per capita ↑	Ecuador: Banana growers paid ↓ $ by intermediaries
	India: Annual 6% economic ↑ /. opening its economy in the 1990s	El Salvador: Salary cut (57¢ → 33 ¢) — clothing factory worker
		Uganda: Banana growers paid ↓ $ by intermediaries ∴ children forced to leave school & left starving X ↑ prices ∵ corporations could buy from other cheaper sources

Task 2
Identify common note-taking abbreviations

The following are some common abbreviations and symbols. What do they mean? Do you think you would be likely to use some of them? If so, which ones? Why? Discuss these questions with your partner for five minutes.

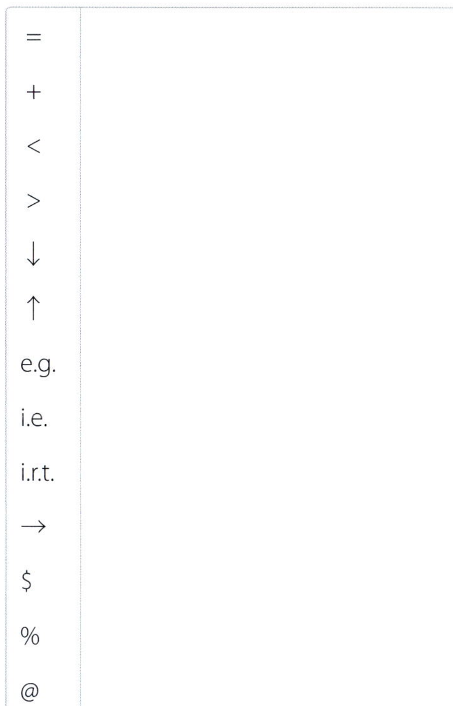

Task 3
Practise note-taking

Imagine that you are reading to prepare for the following essay.

> Describe the rising influence of Western-based food culture in China. Is it a threat?

You have already come up with the following headings for note-taking.

Notes

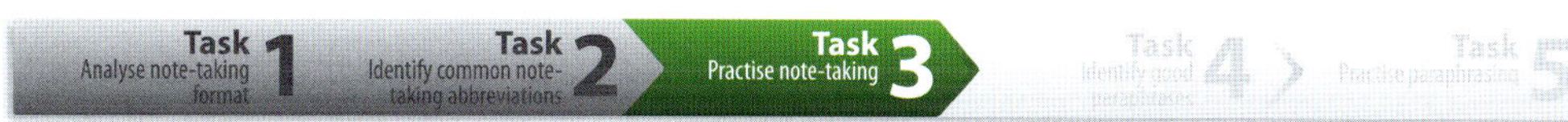

Examples of positive effects of the rising influence of Western-based food culture in China

Spend ten minutes selecting relevant information to include from the following news article. Then make notes. When you have finished, spend five minutes comparing your notes in a small group.

An excerpt of an article written by Celine Sun, entitled "Coffee revolution arrives in China", published in the *China Daily* on 29 November 2010, p. 8.

Despite a long tradition of drinking tea, China's thirst for coffee is surging. According to the China Coffee Association in Beijing, consumption of instant coffee has grown 30% annually in recent years. Last year, Chinese people drank nearly 75,000 tons of coffee, compared with 150,000 tons of tea. Although tea is still the most popular beverage, consumption of coffee is predicted to surpass consumption of tea within three decades.

Coffee was introduced into modern China by Swiss-based coffee maker Nestlé in the 1980s. For many years, it was seen by most Chinese as a high-class gift for friends rather than the daily beverage of personal choice. "There were cases in which people who did not like coffee threw out the coffee but kept the jars to drink tea out of," said Ji Ning, president of the Beijing-based Coffee Association.

In the 1990s, coffee shops started to emerge in big cities, playing an important role in promoting a coffee culture and appealing especially to white-collar workers and expatriates. In the last decade, the circle of coffee lovers has been expanding to embrace the new middle class as well as a much younger group of people born in the '80s and '90s. Coffee shops have given these young people a place to meet and socialize. Culturally, this is drawing teenagers out of the home, which used to be their main source of entertainment, and into a social scene which is very much generation-based. Some see this as a threat to traditional Chinese culture, while others see it as a liberating force for the youth of China.

Ji said instant coffee will, in time, become the dominant product in the China market. On average, a Chinese person currently consumes four cups of coffee weekly but more than twenty cups of tea. The growth potential for coffee in China is huge. Eyeing that vast market, foreign and local companies are bidding against one another for a bigger share of the developing pie.

Starbucks said earlier this year that China will become the second-biggest market behind the US for the company, and they plan to increase the number of mainland stores from 400 to 1,000 in coming years. Hong Kong-based China Resources has also rolled out a plan to open 1,000 more outlets in the country. Fast-food operator McDonald's announced it would add McCafés to 90% of existing restaurants in the country. And Swiss-based food giant Nestlé plans to increase production lines by 75% at its roasting plant in Dongguan, to offer more products domestically.

Paraphrasing from sources

Using the exact words in the original sources without any acknowledgements or quotation marks is plagiarism, a serious academic offence. To avoid this, you must rewrite (or paraphrase) the ideas in your own words. Although this takes more time, **the benefits of paraphrasing are that you can show you have truly understood the ideas** and are **able to present them in your own voice**. **Your paraphrased ideas can also fit in with the rest of your writing in content** (as you can select only the part(s) of a sentence that you need), **vocabulary and style** (as you can choose words that are consistent with the vocabulary and style, e.g. formal or less formal, used in your writing). However, it may not be easy to paraphrase, especially when you have the sources in front of you. The key is to understand the text, **put it away**, and write about the ideas without looking back at the text.

Here are a few tips:

1. In your own words, make notes in point form on the ideas or data while you are reading.

2. Put the original text away, and rewrite your notes into complete sentences.

3. Check the paraphrase to make sure that no important ideas or data are omitted or distorted.

You can **use direct quotes at times when the language in the original source is important**, e.g. some special or technical terms, or statements that are made in very powerful or expressive language and you feel that they cannot be paraphrased. However, direct quotes must be shown in quotation marks and should not be overused in academic writing.

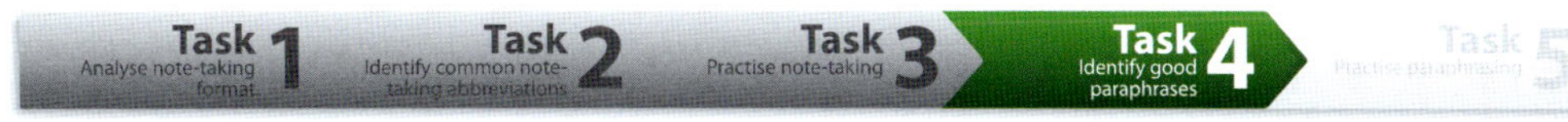

Task 4
Identify good paraphrases

Below are examples of paraphrases written by students. Spend five minutes deciding whether they are good or bad paraphrases, for example whether the student has accurately expressed the ideas in his/her own words. Then spend five minutes justifying your answers with a partner.

Original text

Globalization leads to countries being more connected and interdependent culturally, economically and politically. Economically, it has led to an enormous increase in international trade and investment across different countries, resulting in an increase in wealth and living standards for many countries. For example, the average yearly income per person in China rose from US$1,460 in 1980 to US$4,120 in 1999 ("Change of China's GDP" 2008). However, the gap between the richest and the poorest around the world has increased from 30 to 1 in 1960 to 82 to 1 in 1995 (Purdue 2004). Not all countries, or people within those countries, benefit from globalization equally. In many developing countries, Western companies are maximizing profits by using the cheap labour and raw materials ("Africa: Stand up" 2008). Often, globalization benefits the Western companies, not the people in developing countries.

Source: Hudson, A. (2010). Has globalization improved the living standards in the third world? In S. Edward (Ed.), *Globalization and its effects in the world* (pp. 15–23). London: Johnson Publication.

Paraphrase 1

Countries are now being more connected and interdependent culturally, economically and politically because of globalization. Economically, it has brought about an enormous increase in international trade and investment across different countries, leading to an increase in wealth and living standards for many countries. For instance, the average yearly income per person in China rose from $1460 USD in 1980 to $4120 in 1999.

☐ good paraphrase   ☐ bad paraphrase

Reason: ____

Paraphrase 2

There are both advantages and disadvantages to globalization. According to Houston (2010), increased international trade and investment has improved the living standards in many countries, such as China, which witnessed an increase of income per capita from $1460 USD in 1980 to $4120 in 1999. Nevertheless, Houston points out that not every country gains from globalization in the same way, because in many third world countries, their inexpensive labour and natural resources are being exploited by Western companies.

☐ good paraphrase   ☐ bad paraphrase

Reason: ____

Paraphrase 3

Globalization has improved the economy of some developing countries. An example is China, where average incomes have increased by more than half in just two decades (Houston 2010) as a result of increased trade with and investment by foreign companies. This essay aims to examine the relationships between international trade and the economic growth of China in the past few decades.

☐ good paraphrase   ☐ bad paraphrase

Reason: ____

Paraphrase 4

Globalization often benefits Western companies, not the people in developing countries. The reason is that in many developing countries, Western companies are maximizing profits by using the cheap labour and raw materials ("Africa: Stand up" 2008, as cited in Houston, 2010). This essay will demonstrate that not all countries, or people within those countries, benefit from globalization equally.

☐ good paraphrase   ☐ bad paraphrase

Reason: ____

Task 5
Practise paraphrasing

Use the notes that you made in Task 3—Practise note-taking. Write a paragraph which discusses the positive and negative effects of growth in coffee consumption in China, in no more than 200 words. Remember to acknowledge the source and use a topic sentence. When you finish, ask a partner to give comments and suggest at least one change. This should take you fifteen minutes.

Paraphrase

Citation in tutorial discussions

Using vocabulary for referring to sources of information in discussion

When you discuss a topic in a tutorial discussion, you have to explain **where ideas or data come from** just as you do in your academic writing. It is important to explain that the ideas are not only your own, but they are from good academic sources.

The following are some examples of how you can do this. Can you think of more?

According to an article in the *Journal of Asian Economics* …

I read in a United Nations report that …

Professor Wong from the Centre for Globalization says that …

The WHO put out a report that said that …

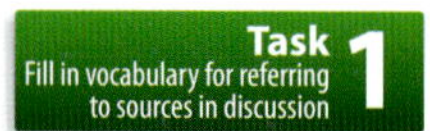

Task 1
Fill in vocabulary for referring to sources in discussion

The following is an excerpt from a tutorial discussion in which students discuss what the best form of economic system is. Fill in each blank with one word that you think is appropriate. When you have finished, compare your answers with your partner and also tell him/her your own view on this topic. Take ten minutes to do this task.

Kelvin	Well, __________ to what I've read, it seems capitalism has worked well for some countries like the US for the past 200 years, but perhaps it's time for change. For example … I read an article __________ by an economics professor from the University of London which said that in a free-market economy … citizens' lives are not well protected … ermmm … if everything is decided by the market. I think this is true during economic recession. The poor suffer but the rich just get richer. So … perhaps there's a need for a stronger government to decide policies that can be more beneficial for the citizens.
Mike	Hmm … do you think it's better to switch to socialism, like democratic socialism?
Rachel	Sorry, what's 'democratic socialism'?
Mike	Well, in this article by Roberts __________ 2002 … in a democratic socialist society … the government owns all the means of production and then distributes the goods or products equally … as much as possible … to everyone. I think this is done through a democratic system, that is, the government is elected by the people and made up of more than one political party.

Judy	Hmm … then, can we say Singapore is a democratic socialist society?
Kelvin	No, I think Singapore is a purely capitalist society, because it has a very open market economy and it attracts lots of foreign investment.
Judy	Yes, but I think capitalism refers to the fact that everything is fully decided by the market itself, like prices of goods, demand, supply, and workers' pay. Well, I got this idea _____________ a book called *Macroeconomics* by a Dr Roberts. But I think in Singapore the government does create policies for the poor, like government housing, right?
Mike	Well … perhaps China is a better example of a democratic socialist system, isn't it?
Rachel	But China doesn't have an election of the government.
Mike	Hang on! There's some kind of election … the members of the National People's Congress … they're elected by provincial officials.
Rachel	But I think China fits very well in the category of Communism, because the term 'Communism' is used to refer to the rule of a single party … that is the Communist Party, and this party decides the economic policies and owns the production of resources … well, I think that is right from listening to yesterday's lecture _________ Professor Chan …
Kelvin	Well, let's get back to our discussion topic then. Which of these systems do you think works best?

Homework
Prepare for a tutorial discussion

In the next tutorial discussion you are going to discuss the following topic.

Is globalization good or bad for poor people?

1. Search for information on Google Scholar and the library electronic databases for at least one written text on this issue. Read the text.

2. Also, use YouTube Education, and watch at least one lecture on this topic.

3. Take notes from what you read and listen to. Note down your own opinions on this topic.

4. Remember, you will need to express the written language as spoken language.

It should take you two hours to do this homework.

Academic Speaking

Transforming written language into spoken language for tutorial discussions

In seminars, you are expected to present and discuss both facts and opinions about a particular topic. To do so, you need to read academic texts for your discussion.

However, students often make the mistake of reading aloud directly from written sources in a tutorial discussion. This is very difficult for the other students to understand. It is very important to transform written language into spoken language by gaining an understanding of the information before presenting the ideas and data in the tutorial. There are a few tips for doing this.

Read the text and make notes on relevant ideas and data. Then think about how you could explain the ideas and data in a simpler way by

- using your own words and not reading directly from the text

- simplifying the grammatical structure

- explaining complex vocabulary or technical terms in simple language

- using signposts to break up long detailed information such as 'the first/second/third point', etc.

- using stress and pausing in your voice for emphasis

Task 1
Transform written language into spoken language

Read the following definition of the term 'protectionism' (an important concept related to globalization). Then make notes about how you would transform the written text into spoken language. Discuss your notes with a partner when you have finished. It should take you ten minutes to do this task.

Protectionism

"Protectionism refers to the imposition of barriers to international trade by government entities. These barriers usually involve either taxes on imports — that is, tariffs — or quantitative restrictions limiting the volume of legally allowable imports of particular goods — or quotas — to achieve various economic and political targets." (p. 247)

Taken from: *Globalization: Encyclopedia of trade, labor and politics, Volume 1*

Task 2
Transform written language into spoken language

Below are definitions of different forms of government around the globe. Your teacher will identify one text for you to transform from written to spoken language using the skills introduced above. Make notes below in point form (don't write out a script; you would just be putting it back into writing). Practise explaining the ideas in spoken language with someone who used the same text. Use a dictionary if you need to. It should take you fifteen minutes to do this task.

Text 1: Monarchy

A monarchy is a governmental system in which sovereignty of a state is held by one single person, the monarch, who is considered to be the permanent head of state. Monarchy originated in the 16th century when new nation-states were formed. The notion that the monarch represented the rule of God formed the basis of unlimited power endowed on him and his inheriting successors, a system referred to as absolute monarchy. The term has, however, evolved to include a political system in which the hereditary head of state acts as a symbolic head, as his power is confined by a constitution that mostly employs a parliamentary system headed by a prime minister. This form of government is called constitutional monarchy, as typified by the monarchy in the United Kingdom.

Source: *The Encyclopedia of Political and Social Sciences*, Volume 1, p. 76.

Text 2: Communism

The term 'Communism' was originally used to refer to a social movement advocating the collective ownership of all means and outcomes of production by everyone in society, culminating in the abolition of class and state. Resources and manufactured products are distributed equally among all members of society, and political and economic decisions are made collectively by means of free participation of every member of society. In modern usage, the term is often used to refer to the government of a state by a Communist party, which typifies the rule of a single party centrally planning the economy and owning all means of production such as state-controlled factories. Current examples of this are China, North Korea, Cuba and Vietnam, although they do vary in their extent of adherence to communist ideology.

Source: Williamson, T. (1995). *Economic politics: The rise of Communism*. Camford: Camford University Press, p. 59.

Text 3: Democratic socialism

The latest edition of *Webster's Third New International Dictionary* defines 'socialism' as a political theory that "advocates collective or governmental ownership and administration of the means of production and distribution of goods". The term is often used in contrast to 'capitalism', which "advocates private ownership for the administration of the means of production and distribution of goods". The dictionary defines a 'social democrat' as "one who advocates a gradual and peaceful transition from capitalism to socialism by democratic means". Volume XV of the *Oxford English Dictionary* defines 'democratic socialism' as "a socialist system achieved by democratic means" and a 'social democrat' is "a member of a political party having socialistic views".

Source: Roberts, M. (2002). Democratic socialism: A note on terminology. *Current Sociology*, *22(4)*: 6.

Text 4: Capitalism

Capitalism is an economic system in which the means of production are owned and operated by private businesses for the purpose of generating profits. The supply of and demand for goods are wholly determined by a free market in which governmental intervention is kept to a minimum. Profits belong to owners who invest in businesses, and wages are paid to workers. Prices of goods and wages for workers are driven by market forces. There are two main benefits to such a system. First, it encourages competition, which in turn drives prices down. Second, it provides incentive for participation in economic activities and development.

Source: Roberts, J. (1999). *Macroeconomics*. Boston: International Press, p. 52.

Task 3
Practise explaining information gathered from your reading

Now, imagine that you are in a tutorial discussion about different forms of government. Explain your form of government to the group and evaluate it. Do you agree with this form of government, or disagree with it? Discuss all of the forms of government as a group. After everyone has finished, give feedback to each other on whether the information was understandable. This discussion should take you fifteen minutes.

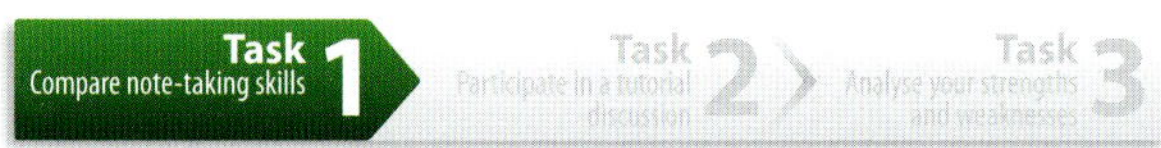

Academic Speaking Tutorial

Task 1
Compare note-taking skills

Look at the notes that your partner took for the homework task on page 63. Answer the following questions.

1. Do you think your partner chose good sources of information?

2. Do you think he or she has enough ideas or data in order to participate well in the tutorial discussion?

3. Does your partner have a clear stance of his or her own?

4. Has she or he thought about how to transfer the written information into spoken language?

It should take you ten minutes to do this.

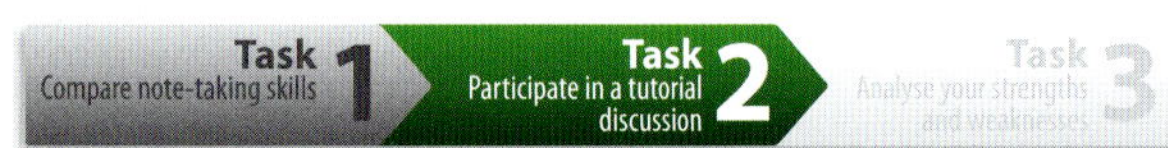

Task 2
Participate in a tutorial discussion

Hold a tutorial discussion for thirty minutes. Remember to:

1. use ideas/data from the text to support your opinions

2. transform written language from the texts into spoken language

3. speak naturally rather than read directly from the text

4. use citation vocabulary when necessary to strengthen the evidence you use to support your own opinions

Task 3
Analyse your strengths and weaknesses

Take five minutes to fill in the form below.

<table>
<tr><td colspan="4">Tutorial Discussion Feedback Form</td></tr>
<tr><td>I found enough information from my own research to discuss the topic in depth.</td><td>☐ Yes</td><td>☐ No</td><td>☐ Sometimes</td></tr>
<tr><td>The sources of information I found from my own research were all academic sources.</td><td>☐ Yes</td><td>☐ No</td><td>☐ Sometimes</td></tr>
<tr><td>I integrated the information from my reading into the discussion to support my arguments.</td><td>☐ Yes</td><td>☐ No</td><td>☐ Sometimes</td></tr>
<tr><td>My ideas were clearly expressed.</td><td>☐ Yes</td><td>☐ No</td><td>☐ Sometimes</td></tr>
<tr><td>I was able to express myself without frequent hesitations.</td><td>☐ Yes</td><td>☐ No</td><td>☐ Sometimes</td></tr>
<tr><td>I know enough vocabulary to be able to express my thoughts and opinions.</td><td>☐ Yes</td><td>☐ No</td><td>☐ Sometimes</td></tr>
<tr><td>I expressed my agreement with others' ideas.</td><td>☐ Yes</td><td>☐ No</td><td>☐ Sometimes</td></tr>
<tr><td>I expressed my disagreement with others' ideas when necessary and gave reasons.</td><td>☐ Yes</td><td>☐ No</td><td>☐ Sometimes</td></tr>
<tr><td>I helped develop some kind of agreement/consensus when possible.</td><td>☐ Yes</td><td>☐ No</td><td>☐ Sometimes</td></tr>
<tr><td>I helped maintain good group relations by being polite, listening to others, showing understanding and not interrupting.</td><td>☐ Yes</td><td>☐ No</td><td>☐ Sometimes</td></tr>
</table>

Ideas for future improvement

Finding and expressing your stance for your assignments

Answer these questions about Unit 3 with your partner.

1. What is a stance?

2. What kinds of academic text would usually contain a stance?

3. How can you make your stance convincing?

Learning outcomes

By the end of this unit, you should be able to:

- identify stance in introductions, conclusions and topic sentences;
- identify biases in a text;
- use hedging words and phrases to express your stance in writing and speaking;
- agree and disagree with the stance of others; and
- use questions to prompt others to think more deeply in a tutorial discussion.

Overview of Unit

As a university student, you are expected to understand a wide range of issues which have a profound impact on the world in the 21st century. These issues may be related to science, business, ethics, politics, or other areas. While you are completing your courses, you will need to do more than just learn about these issues. You will also be expected to **form a well-thought-out opinion** about them. Your opinion about an issue is often called your **stance**.

You can only form your own stance after you have done enough reading about the topic and gathered enough information about it. We talked about this in Unit 2. Unit 3 focuses on how you take the information you have gathered and use it to express your stance. Once you have decided on your stance, you have to be able to communicate this clearly in your writing and speaking assignments. This unit looks at how **you express your stance through language**.

Exploring what stance is

Task 1
Express your stance

What is your stance in relation to these two important issues in the 21st century?
Discuss your opinion with your partner. It should take you ten minutes to do this.

1. The use of sweatshops in developing countries

2. The use of chemicals and genetic modification in the food industry

Expressing stance

Mike and Jane have two very different stances on the issue of sweatshops.

Look at different ways they express stance. As you read through the table, you can see that the stances get much more detailed, clearer and better justified.

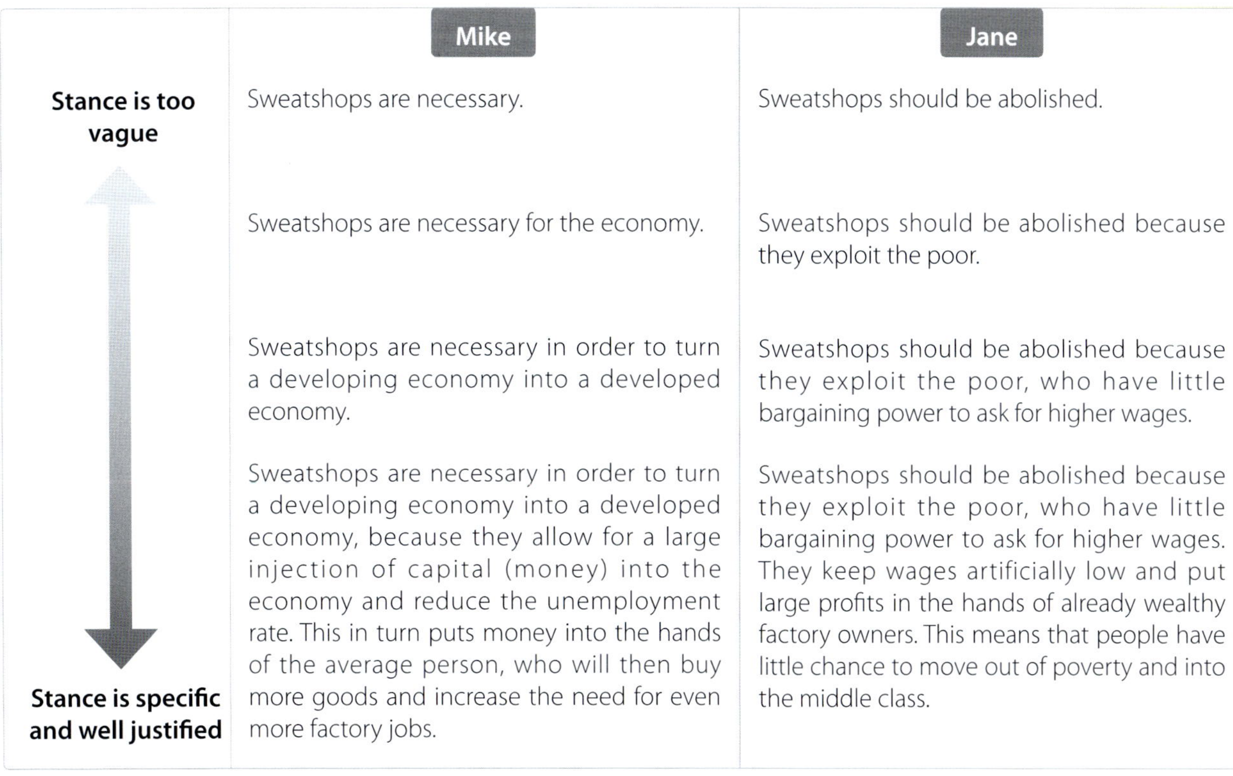

	Mike	Jane
Stance is too vague	Sweatshops are necessary.	Sweatshops should be abolished.
	Sweatshops are necessary for the economy.	Sweatshops should be abolished because they exploit the poor.
	Sweatshops are necessary in order to turn a developing economy into a developed economy.	Sweatshops should be abolished because they exploit the poor, who have little bargaining power to ask for higher wages.
Stance is specific and well justified	Sweatshops are necessary in order to turn a developing economy into a developed economy, because they allow for a large injection of capital (money) into the economy and reduce the unemployment rate. This in turn puts money into the hands of the average person, who will then buy more goods and increase the need for even more factory jobs.	Sweatshops should be abolished because they exploit the poor, who have little bargaining power to ask for higher wages. They keep wages artificially low and put large profits in the hands of already wealthy factory owners. This means that people have little chance to move out of poverty and into the middle class.

Their first attempts at expressing their stance are vague. As you read through the table, you can see the stance is getting clearer and better justified.

Task 2
Express stance in writing

Write a stance for Mike and Jane which expresses two different beliefs about the use of chemicals and genetic modification in food. Make sure the stance is specific, detailed and well justified. It should take you ten minutes to do this.

Stance is specific and well justified	**Mike: supports the use of chemicals and genetic modification in food**	**Jane: opposes the use of chemicals and genetic modification in food**

Task 3
Analyse the language of stance

Look at the following paragraph about sweatshops. Underline the words and phrases which show the author's stance. This should take you five minutes.

> Sweatshops are common in most developing countries. Many people in these countries see life working in a factory as an escape from poverty and an opportunity to get away from life in a rural area, where they would work in harsh conditions on the land. However, life in a sweatshop can be equally harsh. Working hours and conditions can be inhumane, and human rights violations are often frequent (see Long 2010; Edwards 2005; McMillan 2009 for examples). Levels of depression are becoming more and more worrying in many large factories (Swanson 2008). There are, of course, some factories that take the welfare of their workers seriously and sacrifice profits to provide workers with a better standard of living (Yan 2008). This is now more common in the Guangdong area, where media campaigns have educated many workers to fight for their rights and there is some government oversight. However, as a large number of factories move away from the Guangdong area to the northwest of China, human rights violations can be more hidden from the media, and suffering quite often goes unnoticed.

The language of stance

When you are expressing your stance in academic writing, it should appear to be **rational**, not based only on emotion, but **balanced**, **appropriately complex** and **well supported**. When you do this, you sound impartial and less biased. We do this through language in four main ways.

1. Stance should be rational

This is often done by moving the language of opinion away from personal feelings and 'hiding' it in more objective-sounding adjectives, nouns, verbs or phrases. Look at these pairs of sentences.

Opinion/stance is attached to a person (author or person)	Opinion/stance is more objectively expressed
I think that sweatshops are terrible places with a lot of suffering and no one cares.	Suffering can go unnoticed.
Workers are very depressed.	Levels of depression are high.
The factory owners don't care about the workers and make them work long hours.	Working hours and conditions can be inhumane.

Task 4
Identify words which express stance

From the paragraph above, list examples of nouns, adjectives, verbs and phrases which show stance. Take five minutes to do this.

---

2. Stance should be 'hedged' when necessary to make it less open to argument/attack

This is done by using hedging words. The following sentences show the hedging words in bold. Compare these pairs of sentences.

Opinion/stance is not hedged and easy to argue against.	Opinion/stance is hedged and is more balanced and less easy to argue against.
***All** people in these countries see life working in a factory as an escape from poverty, an opportunity to get away from life in a rural town, **always** working in harsh conditions on the land.*	***Many** people in these countries see life working in a factory as an escape from poverty, an opportunity to get away from life in a rural area, **often** working in harsh conditions on the land.*
*Working hours and conditions are **always** inhumane; human rights violations are **always** frequent.*	*Working hours and conditions **can** be inhumane, and human rights violations are **often** frequent.*
*However, as **all** factories move away from the Guangdong area to the northwest of China, human rights violations are **all** more hidden from the media, and suffering **always** goes unnoticed.*	*However, as a **large number** of factories move away from the Guangdong area to the northwest of China, human rights violations **can** be more hidden from the media, and suffering **quite often** goes unnoticed.*

Task 5
Identify examples of hedging

Underline the hedging words and phrases in the paragraph above. Take five minutes to do this.

3. **Stance should acknowledge the other side of the argument and therefore the complexity of the issue.**

Issues that you will come across at university are complex. Whatever your opinion is, there will always be people who will disagree with you, often for good reason. To appear balanced in your stance, you need to acknowledge other points of view (often called a **counter-argument**) and show why they are not as important as your own point of view. Look at this example from the text:

> **There are, of course, some factories that take the welfare of their workers seriously and sacrifice profits to provide workers with a better standard of living (Yan 2008). This is now more common in the Guangdong area, where media campaigns have educated workers to fight for their rights and there is some government oversight.** *However*, as a large number of factories move away from the Guangdong area to the northwest of China, human rights violations can be more hidden from the media, and suffering quite often goes unnoticed.

The word 'however' signals to the reader the shift from one point of view to another.

Task 6
Express a counter-argument

Think about your own stance on this issue. What might be a counter-argument? Tell your partner and see if he or she agrees with your stance or with your counter-argument. Try and convince your partner of your own opinion. Take five minutes to do this.

4. **Stance should be well supported by evidence from the reading you have done.**

Support your stance by using citation to show evidence for your opinion. This makes your stance stronger. Look at this example from the text:

> However, life in a sweatshop can be equally harsh. Working hours and conditions can be inhumane and human rights violations are often frequent **(see Long 2010; Edwards 2005; McMillan 2009 for examples)**. Levels of depression are becoming more and more worrying in many of the large factories **(Swanson 2008)**.

Appropriate use of evidence for expressing your stance

Evidence can take the form of specific real-life examples, figures or statistics from reports, research or survey findings, and views of experts. The function of evidence is to make your stance more believable and objective by providing concrete information and views from some kind of authority. However, you need to be careful when providing evidence in your writing. A few guidelines are listed below.

Avoid citing evidence excessively or adjusting your view to suit the evidence you provide.

Your essay or report should not look like only a lot of evidence cited from various sources without your own assessment of the topic. The cited evidence should not be a substitute for your own thoughts or ideas on the topic.

Check the relevance of the evidence.

Is the evidence related to the context of your discussion? For example, does the information refer to a different time from what your discussion focuses on? Is it provided by a relevant and credible source? For example, it is better to cite a food nutritionist rather than a politician when writing about a balanced diet. Similarly, it is more sensible to cite information from a medical study rather than a tobacco advertisement when explaining the dangers of smoking.

Give the source of the evidence.

Use citation and referencing to show where the information came from and therefore how appropriate it is.

Avoid misinterpretation of statistics.

Avoid using unclear or misleading statistics. For example, when you report increasing or decreasing trends, percentages may overstate the magnitude of the increase or decrease. In this case, it would be more sensible to show the actual figures. This is just one example of the misuse of statistics.

Homework
Practise expressing your stance in writing

Write a paragraph which expresses your stance on the use of chemicals and genetic modification in food. You should include:

- the language of opinion;

- appropriate hedging;

- an acknowledgment of the other side of the argument;

- some 'hypothetical citation' in appropriate places.

It should take you no more than one hour to do this.

Academic Reading

Recognizing and understanding stance while reading

Task 1
State your opinions

Imagine that you can go forward in time to before your future children (one male and one female) are born. At this time in the future, before every child is born, parents are given a 'menu' of traits and abilities that they can choose from for their children. However, they are able to choose only five.

Look at the menu below. Choose five traits for your female child and five for your male child. Discuss your choices with the person next to you. This task should take you ten minutes.

'Mental' traits	Physical characteristics	'Athletic' traits	Personality traits
mathematical ability	hair colour	strong upper body	friendliness
musical ability	eye colour	strong lower body	studiousness
artistic ability	height	good balance	dependability
ability to be empathetic	weight	flexibility	self-confidence
spirituality	body type	good coordination	sociability [this is like being outgoing or being friendly]
ability to be loving	skin colour	good endurance	sensitivity
good memory	ability to age well	fast explosive power [ability to run fast]	independence

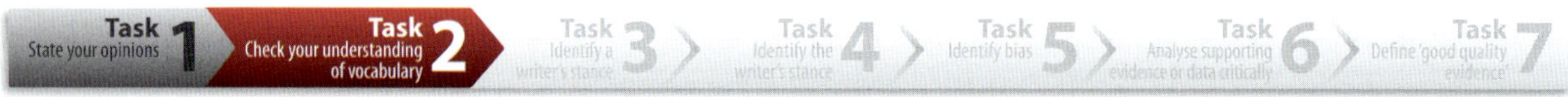

Task 2
Check your understanding of vocabulary

Match the words with their meanings or synonyms. These words are used in Text A below. Check your answers with the person next to you. Use a dictionary if you are not sure. This task should take you ten minutes.

Word		Meaning
1. fertility (n)		A. take something away from someone
2. affluent/well-off (adj)		B. get rid of
3. deprive (vb) someone of something		C. diseases that are passed on from one generation to the next in a family
4. manipulate (vb)		D. before birth
5. eliminate (vb)		E. wealthy
6. genetic screening (n)		F. the ability to produce children
7. notion (n)		G. are given (certain qualities) by birth
8. antenatal (adj)		H. testing the genetic makeup of an organism to see if it is normal or not
9. are endowed (vb) with		I. change something in a way that is of benefit to oneself
10. hereditary (adj) diseases		J. idea, concept

Understanding the writer's stance in reading

Most academic texts have **a stance**. This stance is sometimes very clearly stated but sometimes less obvious. You might have to read carefully to find it. If the stance is explicitly stated, it is usually **given towards the beginning of the text** (e.g. in an introduction, a summary, and an abstract) **and restated at the end**. The writer then **explains and supports his or her stance throughout the text**.

These are just general patterns; you will find texts that do not conform to these exact guidelines.

In order to have a general understanding of the stance of the writer, you can usually:

– read the introduction or summary or abstract of the text

– read the conclusion

– read the topic sentence of each paragraph or the headings and subheadings of sections

Task 3
Identify a writer's stance

First, read only the introduction, conclusion and topic sentences of Text A. Answer the questions below. Once you have done that, read the whole text. Check your answers with the person sitting next to you.

Text A is a student's essay on the following topic:

> Evaluate the ethical issues surrounding the genetic modification of embryos

Answer the following questions in your own words. Do not copy the exact wording from the text.

- What is the writer's stance on the issue of 'designer babies'?

- What reasons does he put forward to support his stance?

- Are there any counter-arguments? If so, what are they?

- Do you agree with his stance? Why or why not?

It should take you ten minutes to do this.

Write your answers in the box and then spend ten minutes discussing your answers with a partner.

Text A: Student essay

The Ethics of 'Designer Babies'

1. Ever since the human genome was successfully decoded in 2003, DNA sequencing technologies have been an increasingly popular area of research. As a result of the ability of technology to map out any person's entire DNA sequence, it is likely that scientists will be able to identify specific genes that account for certain personal attributes, e.g. physical traits, personality, and abilities. Couples will then be able to choose desirable traits for their children with the application of DNA technologies. Some people believe that some degree of antenatal genetic control should be used to improve humankind. However, this essay argues that antenatal genetic selection is unwise, for social and ethical reasons. It will first consider arguments that support these technologies and then discuss the ethical problems concerned.

2. It seems that antenatal genetic control can be used to treat certain diseases. For example, Wesley (2007) suggests that antenatal genetic screening should be used to prevent genetic diseases such as sickle-cell anaemia and cancer. This can be achieved by screening the genetic makeup of human embryos. Only embryos that are healthy are implanted in the mother's womb. Those that carry the genes responsible for causing these hereditary diseases are discarded and used for further scientific research into curing these diseases. It is said that this can help eliminate hereditary diseases in the future generations of a family. The same kind of screening technology can also be applied to help couples have children with specified traits (Green 2006). In the future, as genetic technologies mature, it is possible for parents to exercise even greater control by deciding other attributes of their children such as appearance, personality and intelligence.

3. However, there are serious ethical concerns over the notion of producing 'designer children'. The first criticism points to social inequality. It is likely that only the affluent will be able to afford the huge expense involved in enhancing the genetic makeup of their offspring. The less well-off would have no access to these technologies and might have to accept certain less desirable qualities in their children. This may lead to greater inequality in society, when the rich are endowed with better health and attributes at birth and have greater chance of success in various aspects of life.

4. Another concern is that the freedom and worth of an individual would be diminished. Parents could be seen as depriving their children of choice and autonomy through intentionally controlling their biological traits. Since many of these children's qualities could be predetermined according to their parents' own desires, they would be seen as living a life designed by their parents rather than according to their own free will. Also, embryos that do not conform to parents' preferences would be destroyed in the genetic screening process. This may be even more ethically troubling than abortion, because there could be a large number of embryos tested and discarded. Consequently, people would neglect the worth of the life in each embryo.

5. Genetic selection may also lead to endless competition in creating the 'perfect' human being, and this would be undesirable. If, on average, all children are born to possess better qualities than the previous generation had, what is considered good at present would become just average in the future. It would be hard to stop people wanting to create

an even better human race. People should understand that it would be much better for us to accept the qualities given to us by nature. We should consider our talents as gifts rather than something to control. Parental love should be unconditional, regardless of the attributes children are born with (Sandel 2007). Moreover, if we ourselves have 'defects' like being much shorter or much taller than the average person, we will be more able to sympathize with others who are similar.

6. To conclude, it is morally unacceptable for humans to create 'designer babies' using biotechnology. This kind of genetic control would sharpen social inequality, diminish the rights and worth of individuals, and lead to endless competition in creating the best human being. Using technology to manipulate the 'natural order' would lead to undesirable consequences.

References

Green, M. (2006). *Antenatal genetic screening*. London: University Press.
Sandel, M. J. (2007). *The case against perfection: Ethics in the age of genetic engineering*.
     Cambridge, MA: Belknap Press of Harvard University Press.
Wesley, R. (2007). *Human genetics*. New Haven, CT: Yale University Press.

Task 4
Identify the writer's stance

Look at Text B. This is a student's report on the following topic:

> Write a report on Assisted Reproductive Technology (ART), including the different types, risks and some ethical problems it presents.

Scan through the student's report and do the following:

- Highlight or underline the places in the text where the writer's stance is stated.

- Identify examples of the four aspects of stance mentioned above.

- Do you agree with the author?

It should take you ten minutes to do this task.

Text B: Student report

Report on Assisted Reproductive Technology (ART)

1. Introduction

Female infertility is a condition that seriously affects the lives of significant numbers of women around the world. (This is also a painful medical issue affecting men, but this short report will focus only on women.) It is estimated that the rate of infertility in women is between 8% and 12% around the world, which means that it affects about 50 to 80 million women at any one time. Infertility is defined as a condition in which a woman either cannot get pregnant or cannot carry a foetus to full term if she does get pregnant. The solution for many women is the use of Assisted Reproductive Technology (ART).

2. Types of ART

ART can be categorized according to the type of procedure and according to the types of egg that are used.

2.1 Type of procedure

There are three main types of ART [1]: IVF, GIFT and ZIFT. The differences are explained below.

2.1.1 IVF (*in vitro* fertilization)

IVF is a procedure in which a woman's eggs are extracted and fertilized in a laboratory to create an embryo. The embryo is then implanted back into the woman's uterus.

2.1.2 GIFT (gamete intrafallopian transfer)

GIFT involves the transfer of unfertilized eggs and sperm into the fallopian tubes of a woman. A small incision is made in the woman's abdomen, and the eggs and sperm are guided into the fallopian tubes using a fibre-optic instrument, a laparoscope.

2.1.3 ZIFT (zygote intrafallopian transfer)

ZIFT is the transfer of fertilized eggs into the woman's fallopian tubes.

2.2 Types of egg used

ART can also be categorized according to whether the eggs used are from the infertile woman (non-donor) or from a donor and whether those eggs are fresh or frozen. Figure 1 shows the percentage of each type of ART cycle [1]. In the US in 2009, 70% of ART cycles were using fresh non-donor eggs, 18% were from frozen non-donor eggs, 7% were from fresh donor eggs and 5% were from frozen donor eggs.

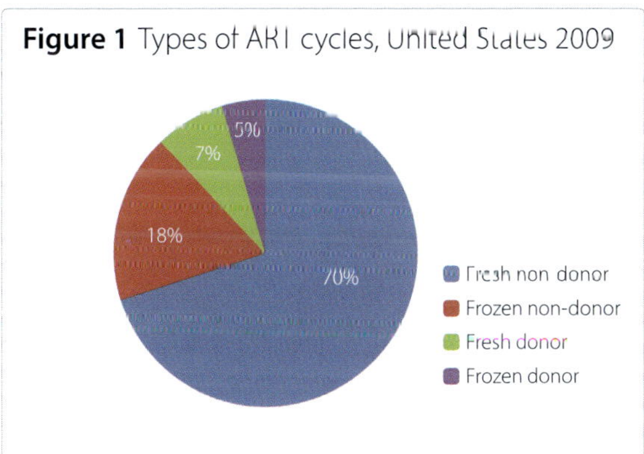

Success rate of ART cycles using fresh non-donor eggs If we take the most common type of ART, using fresh non-donor eggs, we can see that the success rate is relatively low [1]. Only 37% of these ART cycles result in a pregnancy. This is shown in Figure 2.

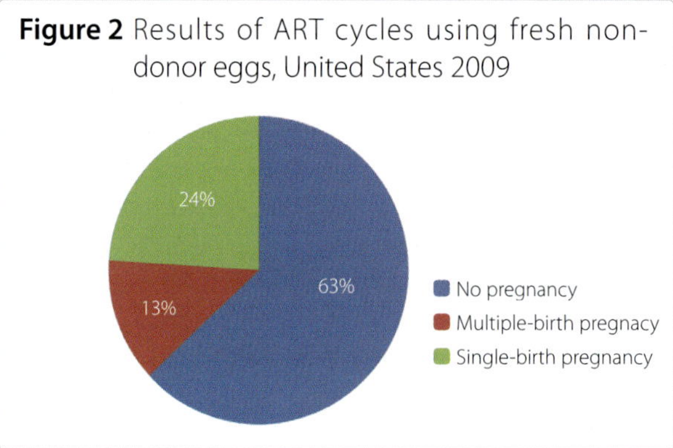

Of that 37%, 82% result in a live birth, and 18% of the 37% result in a miscarriage. Although the medical profession might see this as a relatively high success rate, for many women this is a worrying statistic, especially considering the cost of this treatment.

3. Risks associated with ART

Any medical treatment has some element of risk. However, approximately one million children worldwide have been born through the use of ART. It is important to weigh the risks against the benefits. There are four main types of risk associated with ART [2] for the foetus. They are multiple births, premature births, low birth weight and birth defects.

3.1 Multiple births
Most of the risks mentioned below are associated with the high incidence of multiple births using ART. In the US in 2000, 44.5% of births were twins and 9.3% were triplets. Multiple births are highly correlated with premature birth and low birth weight.

3.2 Premature birth
Premature birth is defined as birth at less than 37 weeks of gestation. The link between premature birth and multiple births can be seen in the following statistics [2]: 92.7% of triplet births are premature, 54.9% of twins and only 6% of single births are premature.

3.3 Low birth weight
Although low birth weight is obviously correlated with multiple births, it is also associated with single births using ART. Research has shown that single births using ART are 2.6 times more likely to be low birth weight than those which are conceived naturally [3].

3.4 Birth defects
Three percent to four percent of natural births have some form of birth defect. The rate for ART-associated births is 1.4–2-fold higher [4]. It is difficult to know the reason for this correlation, as it is complicated by factors such as infertility and the incidence of multiple births.

4. Ethical issues associated with ART

There are many ethical issues with the use of ART. This short report focuses on two main concerns, that of patient autonomy and that of egg donation.

4.1 Autonomy
How much medical freedom a patient should have using ART is controversial. For example, is it acceptable for a woman to request the implantation of several embryos

to increase the chance of getting pregnant but also running the risk of medical complications to the potential foetus(es)? IVF has a much more successful birth rate through multiple-embryo transfer than single-embryo transfer. However, with multiple-embryo transfer, you also increase the risks as described in Section 4. This leads to ethical questions about what appropriate practices should be and who should decide what they are. There has to be some kind of governmental regulation of fertility clinics to ensure that ethical issues are dealt with uniformly — weighing the rights of the recipient of ART and the potential child. For example, the UK requires all fertility clinics to obtain a license from the Human Fertilization and Embryology Authority (HFEA). This licensing system enforces UK and EU laws, which standardize practices across Europe.

There are also issues about whether single women, lesbian couples, menopausal women, etc. should be allowed to receive ART. Many countries, e.g. China, India and Japan, require recipients to be in a heterosexual marriage. The American Society for Reproductive Medicine, however, found no evidence that children are disadvantaged when raised by single or homosexual parents [5]. Prior to 2009, UK fertility clinics had a duty to consider whether a future child needed 'a father' before performing ART. In October 2009, the *Human Fertilization and Embryology Act* was amended to the need for 'supportive parenting' rather than 'a father', and this brought the UK in line with antidiscrimination laws regarding sexual discrimination [6]. In light of the research mentioned above, this seems to be an ethically logical move.

4.2 Donation
There are many ethical issues concerning egg or sperm donation. The issues are largely related to payment for donation and sex selection.

4.2.1 Payment for donation
Most women who use donated eggs acquire them from a family member or a friend. However there is a growing market for 'blind' egg donation, in which the recipient does not know the donor. In Germany, Norway, Sweden and Japan, the use of any form of donor eggs is illegal [7]. However, it was recently reported that one UK clinic has been given permission from HFEA to import eggs from a Russian clinic [8]. If a woman living in poor circumstances is offered a relatively large financial incentive, this potentially hinders her ability to make clear choices. There is a possibility for exploitation of the donor. There has to be some kind of ethical oversight to ensure that this is not happening.

4.2.2 Sex selection
Sex selection is possible through the use of pre-implantation genetic diagnosis (PGD). Many people have strong objections to the use of this technique. For example, the ethics committee of the American Society of Reproductive Medicine advocate that this technology is unethical because, in part, it values one embryo/person over another on the basis of gender [9]. However, couples in the West undertaking PGD are usually doing this for family balancing; for example, they are typically couples in their late 30s with two or three children of one sex and they wish to have a child of the opposite sex [10]. Their wish to use sex selection is not that they value one sex over another but is based on the sex of the children they already have. However, there has been a lot of research documenting gender imbalance in countries such as China and India as a result of sex selection practices (largely a result of abortion or infanticide), so there does need to be ethical oversight in order to determine the purpose for sex selection and to protect against collective harm that would result from widespread sex selection.

5. Conclusion
ART has given millions of women around the world the chance to become pregnant and

have children. Although there are risks associated with ART, it is important to understand the impact this technology has had on the lives of women all around the world for whom having a family is a lifelong goal. Many women experience severe depression as a result of infertility, and medical advancements in this area are the only hope for many of them. It is crucial that more research be done in order to reduce the risks and flesh out legislation to address ethical issues as they arise.

References

[1] Centers for Disease Control and Prevention, American Society for Reproductive Medicine, Society for Assisted Reproductive Technology. 2009. *Assisted Reproductive Technology Success Rates: National Summary and Fertility Clinic Reports*. Atlanta, GA: U.S. Department of Health and Human Services.

[2] Green, N. S. (2004). Risks of birth defects and other adverse outcomes associated with assisted reproductive technology. *Pediatrics* 114:256–9.

[3] Schieve, L., A. S. F. Meikle, C. Ferre, H. B. Peterson, G. Jeng, & L. S. Wilcox. (2002). Low and very low birth weight in infants conceived with use of assisted reproductive technology. *New England Journal of Medicine* 346:731–7.

[4] Mitchell, A. A. (2002). Infertility treatment—more risks and challenges. *New England Journal of Medicine* 346:769–70.

[5] The Ethics Committee of the American Society for Reproductive Medicine. (2009). Access to fertility treatment by gays, lesbians, and unmarried persons. *Fertility and Sterility* 92: 1190–3.

[6] Elliston, S. 2009. The HFE Act 2008 — an end or a beginning? *Bionews* 530.

[7] *Assisted reproductive technologies: Analysis and recommendations for public policy*. (1998). New York: The New York State Task Force on Life and the Law, p, 237.

[8] Hyder, N. (2010). UK clinic granted permission to buy 'Russian eggs'. *Bionews* 586.

[9] Ethics Committee of the American Society of Reproductive Medicine. (1999). Sex selection and preimplantation genetic diagnosis. *Fertility and Sterility* 72: 595–8.

[10] Savulescu, J. & E. Dahl. (2000). Sex selection and preimplantation diagnosis. A response to the Ethics Committee of the American Society of Reproductive Medicine. *Human Reproduction* 15(9):1879–80.

Reading critically: Identifying biases in opinions and data

When you read the opinions of other writers on a certain issue and the supporting data given to support these opinions, you will need to ask yourself whether these opinions or data are **believable** or **likely to be biased**. You may use the following questions to help you decide.

About the author

Is the author or the institution/organization a qualified authority? (You will need to check the credentials of the author.)

Is the author or the institution/organization likely to have vested interests in the issue? (e.g. A tobacco company is likely to hide the dangers of cigarette smoking.)

About the purpose of the text

- Is the text written to inform, explain, or give facts?

- Is the text written to sell or entice?

- Is the text written just for fun, or to entertain?

- Is the language emotional?

- Is the text (website) sponsored by commercials?

Task 5
Identify bias

Your teacher will show you a website. Identify any possible biases and write them in the box below. Work with the person next to you. It should take you five minutes to do this.

| Task **1** State your opinions | Task **2** Check your understanding of vocabulary | Task **3** Identify a writer's stance | Task **4** Identify the writer's stance | Task **5** Identify bias | Task **6** Analyse supporting evidence or data critically | Task **7** Define good quality evidence? |

Task 6
Analyse supporting evidence or data critically

Discuss with a partner whether the evidence or data given in the following examples is believable or not. Also discuss the reasons why. The first one is done as an example. Take ten minutes to do this task.

Example 1

The world has become more interconnected in the last decade. This is shown by the sharp increase in labour migration across countries in the 1980s (Chen 2008).

☐ evidence/data believable   ☑ evidence/data not believable

Reason: The evidence cited refers to the 1980s. It cannot be used to show what has happened in the last decade. In other words, the evidence cited does not apply to the time that the discussion points to.

Example 2

There has been a growing trend of wealthy Asian parents sending their children abroad for further education. In 2006, Germany had the largest number of students learning abroad (Stewart 2007).

☐ evidence/data believable   ☐ evidence/data not believable

Reason: ____

Example 3

A report indicates that income disparity between nations is narrowing.

☐ evidence/data believable   ☐ evidence/data not believable

Reason: ____

Example 4

A survey conducted by Hong Kong University (2008) indicated a drastic increase of 200% in the number of exchange students on campus (from two students in 2005 to four students in 2007).

☐ evidence/data believable   ☐ evidence/data not believable

Reason: ____

Example 5

According to a United Nations report in 2003, 30 low 'human development' countries were in southern Africa.

☐ evidence/data believable   ☐ evidence/data not believable

Reason: ____

Task 7
Define 'good-quality evidence'

Discuss with a partner what makes good-quality evidence. Complete the following table with a few adjectives. It should take you five minutes to do this.

Good-quality evidence should be:

-
-
-
-
-

Homework
Apply skills to another course

Write an analysis of the stance in a text from one of your courses. You should write about:

- the type of text it is
- the author's stance
- the reasons you know this (give evidence of the type of language that shows this)
- your reasons for agreeing or disagreeing with the stance

Your writing should be about 300 words.

Academic Grammar

Hedging

Read the following statements.

- Humans will be able to live on Mars in the near future.
- Scientists will be able to make clones from dead people in the next decade.
- Antenatal genetic selection deprives children of their own choice and autonomy.
- Genetic engineering is absolutely wrong.
- Green (2007) has no doubt made a mistake in believing that some degree of genetic control is beneficial to humans.

The above statements sound absolute and therefore overly simplistic. When writing an academic argument, we often need to discuss points which are not factual but which we think **might** be true, especially when we put forward **a personal stance**. You need to ask yourself:

– How certain are you?

– Is it a fact or an opinion/belief?

If you are not 100% certain, you can express how **likely** you think these ideas are true, by means of certain words and phrases. This is called **hedging**, and it entails using words such as *may*, *might*, *possibly*, and *probably*. Look at the modified examples below.

- Humans **may** be able to live on Mars in the near future.
- **It is possible** that scientists will be able to make clones from dead people in the next decade.
- Antenatal genetic selection **tends to** deprive children of their own choice and autonomy.
- Genetic engineering is wrong **in many circumstances**.
- Green (2007) **seems** to have made a mistake in believing that some degree of genetic control is beneficial to humans.

To make your stance more believable and reasonable to the reader, you should also consider the following questions:

– Do all people believe this?

– Does this refer to all situations?

– Who believes this?

– According to whom?

– Where did you read/find that opinion?

So, instead of saying *"Humans will be able to live on Mars in the near future"*

it is better to say

Many scientists (Smith 2007; Chan 2008) believe that some humans may be able to live on Mars in the near future.

Task 1
Indicate different levels of certainty in writing

Rewrite the following statement to indicate different levels of certainty. This should take you five minutes.

High ↑ Level of certainty ↓ Low	Certain	Humans will be able to live to the age of 200 in the future.
	Probable	
	Unlikely	

Task 2
Identify hedges in a reading text

Go through Text A in the Reading Section again on pages 81–82. Underline the hedging words in the text. Discuss with your partner how the text would be different without these words.

Make a list of as many different hedging words as you can. Put them into grammatical categories. Take ten minutes for this task.

Nouns	Adjectives
e.g. possiblility	e.g. possible

Adverbs	Modal verbs
e.g. possibly	e.g. may

Verbs	
e.g. seem	

Task 3
Practise using hedging

Rewrite the following sentences using hedging words or phrases. Note that, after you rewrite them, they should be less open to criticism from other people. It should take you ten minutes for this task.

Statements which are too strong for opinion	More believable statements
1. Scientists will be able to extend people's lives by using stem cells to grow new tissues or organs.	
2. I think stem cell research is absolutely wrong.	
3. Food produced from cloned animals is totally safe.	
4. In my opinion, robots will definitely replace humans in handling household chores in the future.	

Writing good topic sentences

Task 1 — Identify effective topic sentences

Task 2 — Rewrite topic sentences

Task 1
Identify effective topic sentences

In the following, you will see the body paragraphs of a short essay entitled "The Advantages and Disadvantages of Genetically Modified Food", written by a student. Look at the topic sentence of each of the paragraphs (at the beginning of each paragraph). Decide which are effective topic sentences in expressing the idea of the paragraph and which are not.

Put a tick in the appropriate box. List the reasons you think they are effective or not. Discuss your answers with a partner. Do this task in ten minutes.

Paragraph 1

To begin with, Balsam pears are a good source of vitamins B and C but are extremely bitter. In fact, a lot of foods with high nutritional value are not tasty. By means of genetic modification technology, the bitter taste in Balsam pears can be removed (Food Standard Association 2003). People, especially children, will then be more willing to eat them and benefit from their high nutritional value …

☐ effective topic sentence   ☐ not effective topic sentence

Reason: ____

Paragraph 2

In addition to changing the taste of food, genetic engineering can enhance the nutritional value of some foods. For example, "Golden Rice" was invented to solve the problem of malnutrition in some developing countries (World Health Organization 2009). In these countries, many children suffer from blindness due to Vitamin A deficiency. To combat this problem, scientists successfully changed some of the genes in ordinary rice to produce rice that has a gold colour (hence its name) and is rich in Vitamin A …

☐ effective topic sentence   ☐ not effective topic sentence

Reason: ____

Paragraph 3

According to a report released by the United Nations, the world population will reach 9.2 billion in 2050, and the food shortage problem is likely to get worse. Genetic engineering seems to be a promising solution to the problem of worldwide food shortages. Through this technology, genetically modified food can have higher resistance to diseases and insects and can grow better under adverse weather conditions. This can boost the food supply in some underdeveloped regions …

☐ effective topic sentence   ☐ not effective topic sentence

Reason: ____

Paragraph 4

However, Gregory (2009) warned that genetically modified food might have some hidden health risks for humans. First, some toxic materials can be produced during the genetic modification process, and they would be harmful to human health when eaten (Gregory 2009). Second, the newly inserted genes can cause allergies in some people (Gregory 2009). Lastly, there have been inadequate tests to monitor the safety of GM food for human consumption (Gene Watch 2009).

☐ effective topic sentence   ☐ not effective topic sentence

Reason: ____

Paragraph 5

Moreover, GM food labelling is costly at the moment. For instance, only food products that contain more than 1% of foreign genetic content are labelled in the UK (Gene Watch 2009). Products that are made from GM foods, such as oil made from GM soybeans, need not be labelled. It is hard for consumers to fully understand the content of the food products they are buying. There should be better government regulation of food labelling so that consumers can make more informed decisions.

☐ effective topic sentence   ☐ not effective topic sentence

Reason: ____

Be written in the writer's own voice and indicate the writer's stance on an issue

It should present the writer's stance (viewpoint) on the issue being argued, rather than someone else's stance or idea. Citation of other people's views should therefore appear in the body of a paragraph as supporting evidence rather than in the topic sentence.

Be relevant to all the main points presented in the paragraph

It should precisely capture all the main points discussed in the paragraph.

Be relevant to the central argument/topic of the essay

It should tell the reader the relationship between the paragraph and the central argument or topic of discussion in the essay.

Provide some transition between paragraphs, where necessary

It may provide some linkage between paragraphs by means of transition words or phrases, e.g. apart from …, another … , in addition, however.

Task 2
Rewrite topic sentences

Rewrite each of the ineffective topic sentences in Task 1, by applying the above-mentioned skills. Make changes to other parts of the paragraphs where necessary. It should take you ten minutes to do this.

Homework
Find texts which present different stances

1. Get into a group with 4–5 other people from your speaking tutorial group.

2. Choose one area of scientific research that has ethical concerns (e.g. human cloning, genetically modified food, animal testing, stem cells research, cryonics).

3. Do some research on this topic in the library together.

4. Find at least eight texts that have a different stance on the topic. They could be journal articles, newspaper articles, magazine articles, book chapters etc.

5. Share the texts between you so that at least 2 people have read each text.

6. Make notes on one A4 piece of paper and bring it to the next tutorial discussion.

Academic Vocabulary

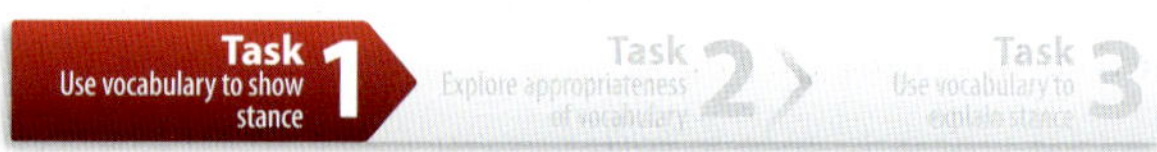

Choosing appropriate vocabulary to show your stance

Task 1
Use vocabulary to show stance

Look at the following issues. Write two mind maps using words which show your own stance on these issues. You can use nouns, verbs, adjectives and phrases. Think about how strong the language is and whether you would want to use some hedging to tone down the strength of the words. Take ten minutes to do this.

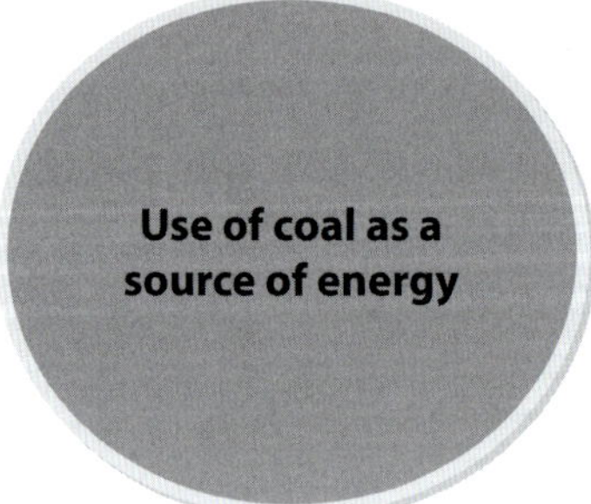

Task 1 Use vocabulary to show stance | Task 2 Explore appropriateness of vocabulary | Task 3 Use vocabulary to explain stance

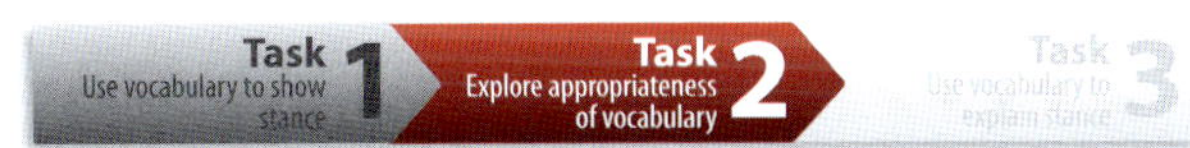

Task 2
Explore appropriateness of vocabulary

While it is important to show your stance, it is also important not to be too 'emotional'. As mentioned, a lot of emotional terminology can make your writing seem biased rather than logical.

Look at the words you came up with on your mind map. Discuss with a partner which ones might sound too 'emotional' to use in academic writing. Which would be more appropriate? Take ten minutes to do this.

Task 1 Use vocabulary to show stance | Task 2 Explore appropriateness of vocabulary | Task 3 Use vocabulary to explain stance

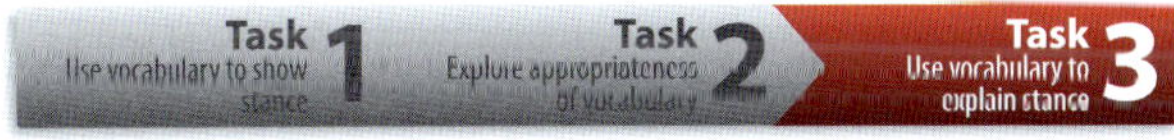

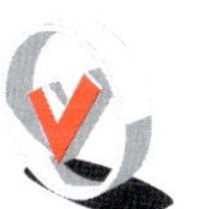

Task 3
Use vocabulary to explain stance

Choose one mind map. Explain your stance about this issue to your partner. Use some of the vocabulary from your mind map. This should take you ten minutes.

Academic Speaking

Expressing your stance in tutorial discussions

As we have discussed, when you are presenting **your stance**, you need to think carefully about how certain you are about this stance and indicate your level of certainty through the use of **hedging words** or **phrases**.

Also, you will need to **support your stance with evidence**. You will need to be able to do this concisely. When you are writing, it is easy to go into detail about the evidence for your stance. When you are speaking, you need to get to the point quickly and clearly.

Finally, in a tutorial discussion, it is important that you **respond to the stance of others**, by **agreeing** or **disagreeing**, and **using questions to prompt others to think more deeply about the issue**.

Task 1
Express your stance

Think about the mind map that you have just used to express your stance. Write down a few sentences which explain your stance. Then, write down the evidence that you would need to back this stance up. Once you have finished, compare your answers with those of the person next to you. It should take you ten minutes to do this.

The first one has been done for you as an example.

Stance	Evidence you would need to back this stance up
The use of coal has no long-term future because it is a finite energy resource.	Research which has predicted when coal is likely to be used up

Task 2
Present and respond to a stance

Pair up with someone sitting next to you. One person should be Student A. The other should be Student B. Choose one of the following ethically controversial topics:

1. Genetic engineering
2. Capital punishment
3. Legalization of drugs
4. Pornography
5. Gambling
6. Euthanasia
7. Use of nuclear energy
8. Polygamy
9. Same-sex marriage
10. Abortion

Student A: You are for
Student B: You are against

Take ten minutes to debate the ethics of your topic. Try to debate continuously by listening to and then responding to each point raised by your partner, without backing down from your position.

Here are some phrases that you can use.

Expressions for presenting your opinion

It seems to me (that) …
I think/believe/feel (that) …
Perhaps …

Expressions for disagreeing with an opinion

That might be true, but
I'm not sure that's true, because …
I see your point, but …
I doubt if that's really the case, because …

Academic Speaking Tutorial

Understanding the importance of asking questions in tutorial discussions

A group discussion is different from an individual oral presentation. In group discussions, participants are expected to not only present their own information and opinions but also to interact with each other by showing agreement and disagreement with each other's ideas.

An aspect that is often neglected by students in a discussion is asking questions to prompt others to think about and discuss an issue more deeply.

You may ask other people for their **opinions**:

How do you feel (about that/it)?

What do you think (about …)?

You may ask **follow-up questions** beginning with a question word such as:

Why … ?

How … ?

Who … ?

Where … ?

You may also use questions that **encourage deeper analysis** of an issue such as:

Is that an important/the most important issue?

Are there other solutions/options?

What can be done better to minimize harmful effects, if the problem cannot be solved completely?

Task 1
Prepare for tutorial discussion

In a moment you are going to discuss your opinions on the topic that you researched for homework last week, an area of scientific research that has ethical concerns (e.g. human cloning, genetically modified food, animal testing, stem cells research, cryonics).

To prepare for the tutorial discussion, spend fifteen minutes thinking about how you will answer the following questions based on the research that you have done. Make some notes in the table below.

What are the main ethical concerns about this area of scientific research?

What evidence is there that these ethical concerns exist?

What do you think should be done about these problems?

Task 2
Participate in a tutorial discussion

Now, hold a tutorial discussion for thirty minutes and discuss the three questions in Task 1 above. Remember to:

1. use ideas and data from the text to support your opinions

2. put written language from the texts into spoken language

3. speak naturally rather than read directly from the text

4. use citation vocabulary when necessary, to strengthen the evidence you use to support your opinions

5. use questions to discuss the issue more deeply

6. use some of the language you practised on page 99 for giving your stance and disagreeing

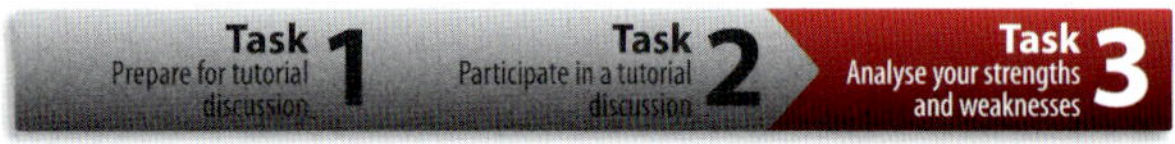

Task 3
Analyse your strengths and weaknesses

Take five minutes to fill in the form below.

Tutorial Discussion Feedback Form

I found enough information from my own research to discuss the topic in depth.	☐ Yes ☐ No ☐ Sometimes	
The sources of information I found from my own research were all academic sources.	☐ Yes ☐ No ☐ Sometimes	
I integrated the information from my reading into the discussion, to support my arguments.	☐ Yes ☐ No ☐ Sometimes	
My ideas were clearly expressed.	☐ Yes ☐ No ☐ Sometimes	
I was able to express myself without frequent hesitations.	☐ Yes ☐ No ☐ Sometimes	
I know enough vocabulary to be able to express my thoughts and opinions.	☐ Yes ☐ No ☐ Sometimes	
I expressed my agreement with others' ideas.	☐ Yes ☐ No ☐ Sometimes	
I expressed my disagreement with others' ideas when necessary and gave reasons.	☐ Yes ☐ No ☐ Sometimes	
I helped develop some kind of agreement/consensus when possible.	☐ Yes ☐ No ☐ Sometimes	
I helped maintain good group relations by being polite, listening to others, showing understanding and not interrupting.	☐ Yes ☐ No ☐ Sometimes	

Ideas for future improvement

Synthesizing your own and others' ideas for your assignments

Test your knowledge

Answer these questions about Unit 4 with your partner.

1. How is a paragraph usually structured in academic writing?

2. Why is the use of pronouns important when you are trying to write a coherent paragraph?

3. Why is it important to be able to describe data in academic writing?

Learning outcomes

By the end of this unit, you should be able to:

- identify main ideas and supporting details in a text;

- use appropriate pronouns to improve coherence in paragraphs;

- group and contrast ideas and/or data from different sources into coherent paragraphs;

- elaborate and support an idea with data; and

- integrate data to support opinions in a discussion.

Overview of Unit

Writing cohesive paragraphs in academic writing

Once you have gathered information for your assignments and have worked out your own stance on an issue, you need to start to put that information together into paragraphs (in essays) and sections (in reports) in your writing. The ability to structure coherent paragraphs and sections is a vital skill for academic writing, as they are the main building blocks of academic writing.

In this unit you will explore what a good paragraph is and how to make it clear, logical, and understandable.

Structuring paragraphs in academic writing

Task 1
Give an opinion

The following three paragraphs are taken from student reports. They are on different aspects of the Chinese economy. Read them. Then decide whether you agree with the stance of the writers. When you have finished, compare your answers with your partner. It should take you five minutes to do this.

Paragraph 1

The poor transportation system throughout China, as well as variations in the availability of good employment opportunities and education, has led to significant variation in regional economies in China. For example, the Pearl River Delta area is extremely wealthy compared to the rest of China. At the time of the 2000 census, this area held only 3.2% of the population of mainland China; however, it contributed as much as 8.7% to the GDP [5]. In contrast, the western area has historically been quite poor. That has been changing, however, with the China Western Development Strategy, which was created by the State Council in 2000 [6]. This has had mixed success. The combined GDP of the western regions has risen from 1.6 trillion in 2000 to 3.3 trillion yuan in 2005 [7]. However, there is still a wide gap between rich people and poor people. The average income of those in urban areas has risen 10% in recent years, whereas it has risen only 2% for those in rural areas [7].

Paragraph 2

Internal migration in China is a complex phenomenon. Poverty in rural areas largely in central and western China leads to a lack of education for much of the population. This lack of education then leads to a lack of employment opportunities for many of the undereducated people (said to be as high as 35% in some rural areas [9]). This in turn causes a large number of people to move to areas such as the Pearl River Delta and large cities such as Beijing and Shanghai to look for work. One-tenth of the 1.3 billion Chinese are said to be internal migrants [10]. These cities then experience high unemployment rates and high levels of homelessness. Finally, all of this can lead to civil unrest (see [11] in Beijing and [12] in Shanghai for examples). Internal migration is a serious destabilizing force in China.

Paragraph 3

There are many systemic problems within the Chinese economy. Corruption is one obvious one. It is very difficult to get exact statistics on the extent of corruption in China, but it is well known that it is widespread and highly damaging to the economy. Another problem is that of underemployment in rural and urban areas. There is a lack of jobs to employ a large percentage of the working population of China, and this can lead to civil unrest. The official unemployment rate for China in 2011 was 4.5%, but it is likely that the number is much higher, sometimes said to be over 20% [12]. It is clear that the socialist aim of a job for all has not been achieved in China although the Chinese government has done a lot in recent years to improve this situation. Finally, there is the high reliance on coal as a source of fuel and the inevitable environmental destruction. Coal was responsible for almost 80% of China's total energy production in 2008 [13]. This is not likely to change if the Chinese government does not stop heavily subsidizing the price of coal.

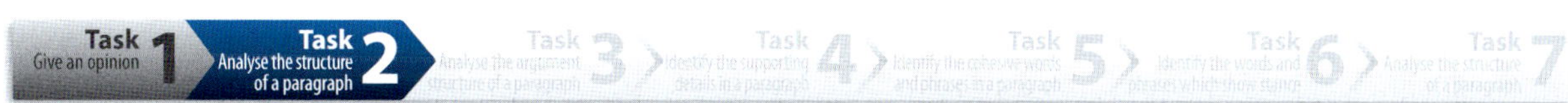

Task 2
Analyse the structure of a paragraph

Look again at the following paragraph. Answer the following question?

How is the argument in the paragraph developed?

Discuss this with your partner for five minutes.

Paragraph 1

The poor transportation system throughout China, as well as variations in the availability of good employment opportunities and education, has led to significant variation in regional economies in China. For example, the Pearl River Delta area is extremely wealthy compared to the rest of China. At the time of the 2000 census, this area held only 3.2% of the population of mainland China; however, it contributed as much as 8.7% to the GDP [5]. In contrast, the western area has historically been quite poor. That has been changing, however, with the China Western Development Strategy, which was created by the State Council in 2000 [6]. This has had mixed success. The combined GDP of the western regions has risen from 1.6 trillion in 2000 to 3.3 trillion yuan in 2005 [7]. However, there is still a wide gap between rich people and poor people. The average income of those in urban areas has risen 10% in recent years, whereas it has risen only 2% for those in rural areas [7].

Elements of good paragraph construction in academic writing
1. The argument in the paragraph should be developed logically.

Task 3
Analyse the argument structure of a paragraph

Read Paragraphs 1 and 2 again. Take note of the words in bold. Then, fill in the gaps in the mind maps to show the argument structure of the paragraph. Take ten minutes to do this.

Paragraph 1

The poor transportation system throughout China, as well as variations in the availability of good employment opportunities and education, has led to **significant variation in regional economies** in China. **For example, the Pearl River Delta area** is extremely wealthy compared to the rest of China. At the time of the 2000 census, this area held only 3.2% of the population of mainland China; however, it contributed as much as 8.7% to the GDP [5]. **In contrast, the western area** has historically been quite poor. That has been changing, however, with the China Western Development Strategy, which was created by the State Council in 2000 [6]. This has had mixed success. The combined GDP of the western regions has risen from 1.6 trillion in 2000 to 3.3 trillion yuan in 2005 [7]. However, there is still a wide gap between rich people and poor people. The average income of those in urban areas has risen 10% in recent years, whereas it has risen only 2% for those in rural areas [7].

Paragraph 1 Mind Map

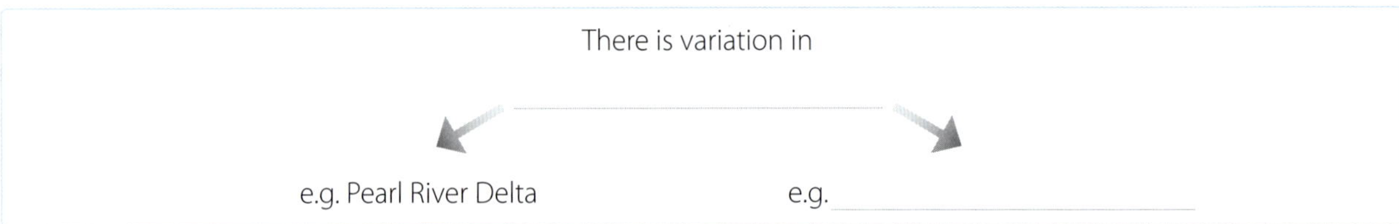

Paragraph 2

Internal migration in China is a complex phenomenon. **Poverty** in rural areas largely in central and western China leads to a **lack of education** for much of the population. **This lack of education** then leads to a lack of employment opportunities for many of the uneducated people (said to be as high as 35% in some rural areas [9]). **This** in turn causes a **large number of people to move** to areas such as the **Pearl River Delta and large cities such as Beijing and Shanghai** to look for work. One-tenth of the 1.3 billion Chinese are said to be internal migrants [10]. **These cities** then experience **high unemployment rates** and high levels of homelessness. Finally, **all of this** can lead to **civil unrest** (see [11] in Beijing and [12] in Shanghai for examples). Internal migration is a serious destabilizing force in China.

Paragraph 2 Mind Map

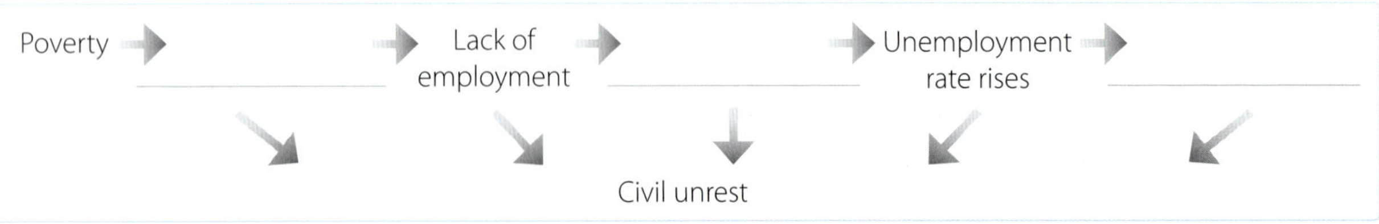

Task 4
Identify the supporting details in a paragraph

The main idea has been highlighted in bold. Underline the supporting details. Take five minutes to do this.

Paragraph 1

The poor transportation system throughout China, as well as variations in the availability of good employment opportunities and education, has led to significant variation in regional economies in China. For example, the Pearl River Delta area is extremely wealthy compared to the rest of China. At the time of the 2000 census, this area held only 3.2% of the population of mainland China; however, it contributed as much as 8.7% to the GDP [5]. In contrast, the western area has historically been quite poor. That has been changing, however, with the China Western Development Strategy, which was created by the State Council in 2000 [6]. This has had mixed success. The combined GDP of the western regions has risen from 1.6 trillion in 2000 to 3.3 trillion yuan in 2005 [7]. However, there is still a wide gap between rich people and poor people. The average income of those in urban areas has risen 10% in recent years, whereas it has risen only 2% for those in rural areas [7].

Paragraph 2

Internal migration in China is a complex phenomenon. Poverty in rural areas largely in central and western China leads to a lack of education for much of the population. This lack of education then leads to a lack of employment opportunities for many of the uneducated people (said to be as high as 35% in some rural areas [9]). This in turn causes a large number of people to move to areas such as the Pearl River Delta and large cities such as Beijing and Shanghai to look for work. One-tenth of the 1.3 billion Chinese are said to be internal migrants [10]. These cities then experience high unemployment rates and high levels of homelessness. Finally, all of this can lead to civil unrest (see [11] in Beijing and [12] in Shanghai for examples). Internal migration is a serious destabilizing force in China.

Task 5
Identify the cohesive words and phrases in a paragraph

Cohesive words and phrases have been bolded in Paragraph 1. Underline them in Paragraph 2. Explain the function of each word and phrase with your partner. Take five minutes to do this.

Paragraph 1

The poor transportation system throughout China, as well as variations in the availability of good employment opportunities and education, has led to significant variation in regional economies in China. **For example,** the Pearl River Delta area is extremely wealthy compared to the rest of China. At the time of the 2000 census, this area held only 3.2% of the population of mainland China; **however, it** contributed as much as 8.7% to the GDP [5]. **In contrast,** the western area has historically been quite poor. **That** has been changing, **however,** with the China Western Development Strategy, which was created by the State Council in 2000 [6]. **This** has had mixed success. The combined GDP of the western regions has risen from 1.6 trillion in 2000 to 3.3 trillion in 2005 yuan [7]. **However,** there is still a wide gap between rich people **and** poor people. The average income of **those** in urban areas has risen 10% in recent years, **whereas it** has risen only 2% for those in rural areas [7].

Paragraph 2

Internal migration in China is a complex phenomenon. Poverty in rural areas largely in central and western China leads to a lack of education for much of the population. This lack of education then leads to a lack of employment opportunities for many of the uneducated people (said to be as high as 35% in some rural areas [9]). This in turn causes a large number of people to move to areas such as the Pearl River Delta and large cities such as Beijing and Shanghai to look for work. One-tenth of the 1.3 billion Chinese are said to be internal migrants [10]. These cities then experience high unemployment rates and high levels of homelessness. Finally, all of this can lead to civil unrest (see [11] in Beijing and [12] in Shanghai for examples). Internal migration is a serious destabilizing force in China.

4. The paragraph should make the stance clear and support this with evidence through citations.

Task 6
Identify the words and phrases which show stance

Words and phrases which show stance have been bolded in Paragraph 1. Underline them in Paragraph 2. Check your answers with your partner. Take five minutes to do this.

Paragraph 1

The **poor** transportation system throughout China, as well as variations in the availability of good employment opportunities and education, has led to **significant** variation in regional economies in China. For example, the Pearl River Delta area is **extremely wealthy** compared to the rest of China. At the time of the 2000 census, this area held only 3.2% of the population of mainland China; however, it contributed as much as 8.7% to the GDP

[5]. In contrast, the western area has historically been **quite poor**. That has been changing, however, with the China Western Development Strategy, which was created by the State Council in 2000 [6]. This has had **mixed success**. The combined GDP of the western regions has risen from 1.6 trillion in 2000 to 3.3 trillion yuan in 2005 [7]. However, there is still a **wide gap** between the rich and poor. The average income of those in urban areas has risen 10% in recent years, whereas it has risen **only** 2% for those in rural areas [7].

Paragraph 2

Internal migration in China is a complex phenomenon. Poverty in rural areas largely in central and western China leads to a lack of education for much of the population. This lack of education then leads to a lack of employment opportunities for many of the uneducated people (said to be as high as 35% in some rural areas [9]). This in turn causes a large number of people to move to areas such as the Pearl River Delta and large cities such as Beijing and Shanghai to look for work. One-tenth of the 1.3 billion Chinese are said to be internal migrants [10]. These cities then experience high unemployment rates and high levels of homelessness. Finally, all of this can lead to civil unrest (see [11] in Beijing and [12] in Shanghai for examples). Internal migration is a serious destabilizing force in China.

Task 7
Analyse the structure of a paragraph

Analyse Paragraph Three using the four elements of good paragraph construction outlined above. This task should take you ten minutes.

Paragraph 3

There are many systemic problems within the Chinese economy. Corruption is one obvious one. It is very difficult to get exact statistics on the extent of corruption in China, but it is well known that it is widespread and highly damaging to the economy. Another problem is that of underemployment in rural and urban areas. There is a lack of jobs to employ a large percentage of the working population of China, and this can lead to civil unrest. The official unemployment rate for China in 2011 was 4.5%, but it is likely that the number is much higher, sometimes said to be over 20% [12]. It is clear that the socialist aim of a job for all has not been achieved in China although the Chinese government has done a lot in recent years to improve this situation. Finally, there is the high reliance on coal as a source of fuel and the inevitable environmental destruction. Coal was responsible for almost 80% of China's total energy production in 2008 [13]. This is not likely to change if the Chinese government does not stop heavily subsidizing the price of coal.

Academic Reading

Identifying main ideas and supporting details

Companies pour a lot of money into brand building and marketing, including newspaper and television advertisements, because they influence consumers' choices tremendously. Shoppers are often affected by the values the advertisements express both explicitly and implicitly.

As a consumer, have you thought about factors that influence the choice you make when you buy an item?

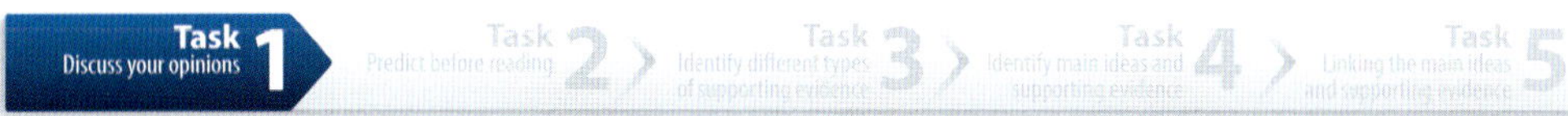

Task 1
Discuss your opinions

Discuss the following questions with your partner. Take ten minutes to do this.

1. What affects your choice when you buy a product?

2. Are there any brands which you are loyal to? Why?

3. Can you remember an incident when you bought a specific product after seeing an advertisement for it?

4. Are you influenced by advertisements?

5. If you were working for a company marketing Chinese herbal tea in the Western world, what brand-building strategies would you recommend? What qualities in the brand would you emphasize?

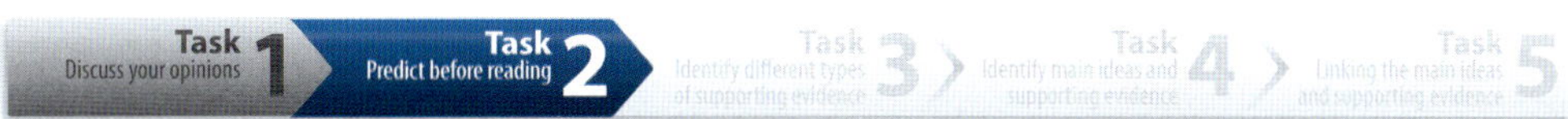

Task 2
Predict before reading

Read the introduction of the text below. Predict what you think the brand-building strategies are of Wang's Fortune Tea and Café de Coral. Take five minutes to do this. Compare your answers with those of your partner.

Brand-building strategies: The case of two successful Chinese enterprises

1   China, once known as the world's factory, used to be happy to provide low-cost labour and produce inexpensive products for the rest of the world. Companies gave little thought to building their brand. However, more and more Chinese enterprises are putting a lot of money and effort into building the reputation of their brand. Small local companies are emerging as national brands by using a number of brand-building strategies, including creating a powerful brand name, positioning themselves in the market and expressing corporate social responsibility. These days it seems that branding is crucial when trying to sell a product. In the following, the strategies of two Chinese enterprises, Wang's Fortune Tea and Café de Coral, show how these companies have used brand-building strategies to maximize profit.

2   One of the most important ways of building a brand is to come up with an attractive and memorable brand name and packaging. An effective brand image leaves a strong impression in the mind of the consumer, thereby increasing the company's competitiveness. Wang's Fortune Tea, a Chinese herbal drink, has focused on Chinese philosophy in its brand building. The Chinese equivalent, *Wanglaoji*, is easy to pronounce and remember. The package is mainly red and yellow, and *ji* in its name means 'fortune'. Both the colour & *ji* have an auspicious meaning to Chinese people, signifying blessings and good luck. This successfully targets the Chinese market.

3   Since 2003, Wang's Fortune Tea has recognized the importance of brand building and marketing. After the outbreak of SARS, Chinese consumers became a lot more health conscious, and this was reflected by their demand for healthier drinks and the popularity of Wang's Fortune Tea. The company responded to this and started promoting the product as a tea that heals internal ailments (Gao, Lu & Fung 2008), resulting in a phenomenal increase of 400% profit compared to pre-SARS years. In fact, to many people herbal teas are becoming more appealing than carbonated soft drinks such as sodas ("Herbal tea," 23 February 2009).

4   Showing corporate social responsibility also has an effect on profits. There are different ways in which a company can express its social responsibility, one of which is corporate philanthropy such as donating time, money, or resources to the community. The Wanglaoji enterprise earned a lot of publicity for donating 100 million yuan to the Sichuan earthquake victims in 2008. This action led to not only higher recognition of the brand and built an image of patriotism, but it also led to its brand value hitting 540 million yuan (Wang 2009). In other words, corporate social responsibility can contribute to brand building and business success.

5   The other example of a successful Chinese enterprise is Café de Coral, a fast-food chain store in Hong Kong. The company is more widely known among locals as *Dajiale*, which literally means 'everybody happy together' and 'everybody' (*Dajia*) in its brand name represents customers, staff and shareholders. The name and the logo (a roof above the three Chinese characters, all in red) has been well known in Hong Kong since the '60s (Cai & Jiang 2008). However, it is not solely the name that helped its business but rather its brand positioning, which is "the standing of a brand in comparison with its competitors in the minds of customers, and other stakeholders" (Duncan 2005: 75). Starting off as a family business, Café de Coral was the first to introduce the pioneering system of payment first and self-service after. It foresaw the decline of in-house catering services in the '70s, due to the need to apply for licenses, and therefore an increase in the demand of eateries for local workers. As an economical fast-food restaurant, it has positioned itself to be efficient with

its service, abundant in choice of meals and high in aspirations. It also put a tremendous amount of profits in their early years, nearly 30%, into television advertising in the '80s, which was a first in the local fast-food industry. Indeed, one of the slogans, "Achieving a hundred percent for you", has successfully been associated with Café de Coral (Cai & Jiang 2008).

6   The above two cases demonstrate the importance of brand building and brand positioning in the competitive Chinese market. It is insufficient to only have an easy-to-remember brand name; each strategy mentioned above affects the brand image. These tactics include how clearly one defines the value of the products in a particular market and how one communicates this to the customers. Although the aforementioned enterprises have become strong regional and national brands, much more can be done to penetrate the global market.

References

Cai, L. & Q. Jiang. (2008). *Achieving a hundred percent for you: The change and development of Café de Coral in the past four decades*. Xianggang: Tian di tu shu.

China Economic Net. (23 February 2009). Herbal tea hot in China. Retrieved on 25 May 2009 from http://en.ce.cn/Industries/Consumen-Industries/200902/23/t20090223_18293299.shtml

Duncan, T. (2005). *Principles of advertising & IMC* (2nd ed.). New York: McGraw-Hill/Irwin.

Gao, G. Y., J. Y. Lu, & H. G. Fung. (2008). *Wang's Fortune Tea from China: Competing for a new arena of the beverage market (A)*. Hong Kong: The University of Hong Kong.

Kotler, P., & W. Pfoertsch. (2006). *B2B brand management*. Berlin; New York: Springer.

Sanders, H. M. (12 August 2008). Blue China it's not. *New York Post*. Retrieved on 16 July 2009 from http://www.nypost.com/seven/08122008/business/blue_china_its_not_124076.htm

Wang, Y. (26 June 2009). Wanglaoji in top list for the first time. *China Daily*. Retrieved on 16 July 2009 from http://www.chinadaily.com.cn/bizchina/2009-06/26/content_8325225.htm

Supporting evidence in paragraphs

As we have discussed, paragraphs in academic writing include **main ideas** and **supporting evidence**.

Main ideas

Main ideas are centrally related to the topic of a text and/or the stance of the writer. They are the most important points that the writer intends to express for a topic.

Supporting details

Supporting evidence develops and supports the main ideas and stance. There are many types of supporting details. They can be facts, statistics, examples, quotations, and expert opinions.

Task 3
Identify different types of supporting evidence

Match the type of supporting evidence with the example. It should take you five minutes to do this. The first one has been done for you.

Facts	The exchange rate, value of a currency and how it fluctuates in relation to other currencies can affect relationships between countries. For example, when China de-pegged the yuan from the US dollar on 21 July 2005, it relieved the Sino-US tension that that had been building regarding the revaluation of the yuan.
Statistics	Pollution in China has become a serious public health issue. "Cancer is now China's leading cause of death as a result of increases in pollution", according to Professor Li, researcher at the Ministry of Health.
Examples	Tighter implementation measures have been employed in trying to achieve zero population growth in China since 1978. The one-child policy was introduced and was enacted in 1979. Under this policy, married couples living in urban areas can have only one child.
Quotations from experts	As we are evaluating the effectiveness of the population control policy in China, it is important for us to understand its historical development. As discussed in a report published by the Laogai Research Foundation (2004), there are three distinct phases. First is the liberal period, which was from 1949 to 1964, during which the Chinese government encouraged childbirth as much as possible. The second phase was from 1965 to 1978, during which voluntary family planning was encouraged. Finally the third phase was from 1979 until the present, during which mandatory population control was enforced.
Expert opinions	In 2003, following SARS and the company's change in marketing tactics and positioning, Wang's Fortune Tea saw explosive growth nationwide and was finally able to break out of its regional image to become a major national brand. In 2006, less than ten years after the drink starting selling nationwide, it became China's top beverage company, having about a 90% market share of the herbal tea industry and sales revenue of US$512.16 million.

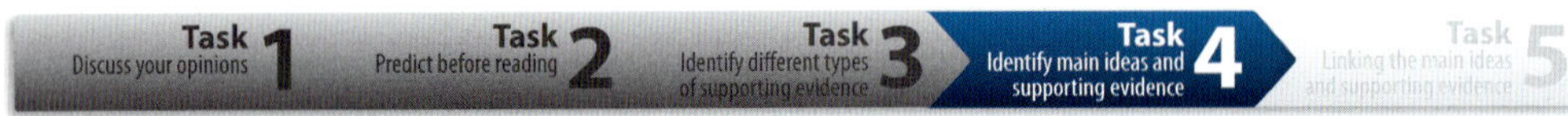

Task 4

Identify main ideas and supporting evidence

Now read the essay above in full. Identify the main ideas and supporting evidence of Paragraphs 2 to 5 in point form. Decide what type of supporting evidence it is, e.g. fact, statistics, example etc. This should take you fifteen minutes.

Paragraph 2

Main idea

Supporting evidence

Paragraph 3

Main idea

Supporting evidence

Paragraph 4

Main idea

Supporting evidence

Paragraph 5

Main idea

Supporting evidence

Task 5
Linking the main ideas and supporting evidence

Read the following paragraphs about Lee Kum Kee (a famous Hong Kong company which specializes in sauces). Write the main idea in the form of a topic sentence for the supporting evidence in the paragraph. Explain your choice to your partner. You should take fifteen minutes to do this task.

1. ____ .
Lee Kum Kee ensures that their products are of the highest quality and have emphasized that quality control is on the top of their priority list ("Old company" 2003; Yiu 2007). Quality control was taken to another level in 1995, when Lee Kum Kee became the first Hong Kong food manufacturer accredited with an ISO9002 Certificate by the Hong Kong Quality Assurance Agency and British Standards Institution (Yiu 2007).

2. ____ .
This has in fact led the business to succeed and expand in its markets. For example, building on the best-liked oyster sauce, new sauces were developed, including one called Panda Oyster Sauce in 1972 and XO sauce in 1992 (Yiu 2004). This XO sauce, which is made from dried scallop, ham and dried shrimp, was a major success for the company ("Old company" 2003) and led to a significant increase in profit them.

3. ____ .
The company has therefore developed a sweetened fish soya sauce just for the local Hong Kong market, to imitate the way steamed fish is cooked in Cantonese restaurants. Another example is that the flavour of the same sauce sold in Beijing and Shanghai is slightly altered to suit different regional tastes ("Old company" 2003). The brand is diversified and the market is expanded substantially through this continual development of new products catering to the needs of different market segments.

Homework
Apply skills to another course

Write an analysis of the structure of two paragraphs (not the introduction or the conclusion) from a text you are reading for one of your other courses. Describe the following for each paragraph:

- how the argument is developed

- what the main idea and supporting details are

- what type of supporting details there are

- what examples of cohesion are in the paragraph

- what examples of language are used to show stance

Do this in less than 300 words.

Academic Grammar

Using pronouns in paragraph structure

Use of pronouns in paragraphs

The following sentences sound repetitive because of there is no use of pronouns.

Extract 1

China is the most populous country in the world. China is also one of the oldest civilizations. China is expected to be one of the leading nations economically in the future because of its rapidly growing economy.

The following sounds less repetitive:

Extract 2

China is the most populous country in the world. It is also one of the oldest civilizations. It is expected to be one of the leading nations economically in the future because of its rapidly growing economy.

The pronouns avoid repetition and therefore link ideas in a paragraph coherently. As shown in the above example, pronouns replace nouns used in an earlier statement, usually in the preceding sentence. Because these nouns appear before the pronouns, they are called **antecedents** ('ante-' means 'before').

'Antecedent' of 'it'

The Pearl River Delta area is extremely wealthy. It contributed as much as 8.7% of GDP.

In the above example, the pronoun 'it' refers to 'the Pearl River Delta area', which is the antecedent of the pronoun.

Quite often, it will be very difficult to follow a pronoun if we cannot locate its antecedent. It must be fairly close to the pronoun for the meaning to be clear.

One common mistake found in students' writing is the confusion between 'it' and 'this'. We use **this** to refer to the **whole idea in the preceding sentence**. We use it to refer to a **single noun**. The following extracts demonstrate this difference.

Example One

Café de Coral was the first to introduce the pioneering system of payment first and self-service after. It foresaw the decline of in-house catering services in the '70s.

Question: What foresaw the decline of in-house catering services in the '70s?
Answer: Café de Coral (it)

Example Two

Café de Coral was the first to introduce the pioneering system of payment first and self-service after. This helped to make its service very efficient.

Question: What helped to make its service very efficient?
Answer: the introduction of the pioneering system of payment first and self-service after (this)

Task 1
Identify pronoun antecedents

Read the following paragraphs. Highlight the pronouns in the paragraph. Then 'track' these pronouns to their antecedents. The first one has been done for you as an example. It should take you ten minutes to do this.

Higher Education in China

Referring to China

China has been experiencing exponential economic growth since the opening up of China's market in the 1970s and it has amazed the world with its growth. Disappointingly, at the same time, it is a country with about one-fifth of the total number of economically deprived people in world. There are approximately 211 million Chinese who are living in extreme poverty [1]. They were living on less than US$1 per day in 2001 [2]. This in turn leads to inequality and huge disparity in the opportunities, educational resources, taxable funding and quality of teachers in both rural and urban schools. These are serious barriers to an improved living standard.

There are more than 200 million students currently studying in Chinese primary and secondary schools. In order to gain university entrance, they must pass exams in English, mathematics, Chinese language and culture. However, the schools in the rural areas cannot attract qualified English teachers. Because of limited resources, they usually cannot afford the expense of hiring a good English teacher. This, to a large extent, often leads to low college entrance rates in rural areas. Only 0.2% of students manage to gain access to university education from these schools.

Task 2
Improve paragraph coherence with pronouns

The following text is slightly incoherent. Rewrite the paragraph using appropriate pronouns and phrases using pronouns, to achieve better coherence. It should take you ten minutes to do this.

There have been some dramatic changes in the higher education system in China over the past sixty years. From 1953 to 1957, the higher education system was heavily centralized and standardized; all the teaching plans, syllabuses, materials and textbooks were unified by the central government. From 1953 to 1957, graduates were allocated to jobs controlled by the state government according to human resources requirements. The human resources requirements were usually decided by government officials. Government officials did not give graduates a choice as to which job or position they could choose. Starting in the late '70s, there have been reforms leading to greater decentralization of education. Local education authorities have taken a leading role instead of the Chinese central government. The Chinese central government instead has become a facilitator and evaluator. Higher education has also become modernized and commercialized. Higher education has largely been shaped by the needs of the business sector.

Academic Writing

Task 1
Identify similarities and differences

Another important skill in academic writing is to show similarities and differences in opinions of main ideas in your reading. This is an important skill in academic writing.

Read the following definitions of *guanxi* from four online sources. Identify the similarities and differences in the four definitions. This task should take you ten minutes.

Definition 1

"Guanxi describes the basic dynamic in personalized networks of influence, and is a central idea in Chinese society." (Chan 2001: 19)

Definition 2

"**Guanxi:** Guanxi is the term often used to express the cultural differences that affect doing business in China vs. the West. Guanxi describes the interplay of a complex network of personal and social relationships. It can be understood as not being just what you know but also whom you know. This is still a central concept in Chinese society." (Leung 1998: 5)

Definition 3

"A Chinese term meaning 'networks' or 'connections,' understood to be a network of relationships designed to provide support and cooperation among the parties involved in doing business. According to the Los Angeles Chinese Learning Center, by obtaining the right guanxi, organizations minimize the 'risks, frustrations, and disappointments when doing business in China.'" (Williams 2007: 156)

Definition 4

"a Chinese social concept based on the exchange of favours, in which personal relationships are considered more important than laws and written agreements" (Manning 2010: 301)

Similarities

Differences

Synthesizing

Synthesizing is an important process in academic writing. When you write an essay or a report, you will have to do a lot of reading. **However, when you do this reading, you will often discover that a lot of the evidence that you find to support your stance is contradictory.**

You can't just ignore this contradictory information. You have to be able to synthesize the evidence into your writing, explain the differences and draw some conclusions about it.

How can you bring different and similar ideas together from different texts into your own writing?

To begin with, we need to *analyse* the sources we are reading and *identify* the main theme, views or comments of each source (e.g. *guanxi* = 'relationship'). We then *compare and contrast* these specific themes, views or comments. After the similarities and differences have been identified, we decide *if* and *how* we can fit these similarities and differences into our own arguments. We need to be *selective* so as to keep the original meaning of the sources and include only the most relevant and suitable details in our writing. The most relevant and suitable details are closely related to our own argument.

The following flowchart summarizes what synthesis is.

Analyse > Identify > Compare and Contrast > Select > Paraphrase and Include

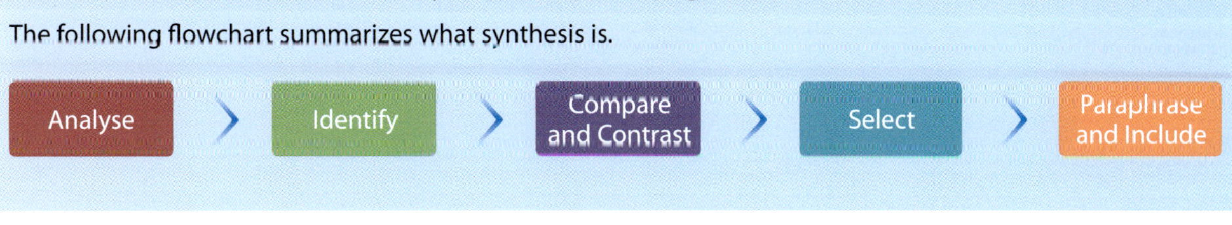

Task 2
Synthesize ideas from different sources

Based on the similarities and differences you have noted in the previous task, write a short paragraph defining what guanxi is. Remember to use appropriate citation techniques in referring to the above sources. When you have finished, compare your paragraph with that of your partner. Suggest at least one change you think he or she should make. Take twenty minutes for this task.

Homework
Synthesize ideas from different sources

Read the following extracts on *feng shui*. Write a 100-word paragraph to explain what *feng shui* is. Remember to refer to the given sources with proper citation techniques.

Extract 1

Feng shui is a Chinese system which people follow in the layout of their homes or offices. The system advises people how to place the furniture, what special objects or displays to place in the homes or offices, and what colour to paint the walls of the rooms. Arrangements made according to the *feng shui* system can presumably bring the occupants happiness, health and wealth. (Wood 2009)

Extract 2

Feng shui is a set of Chinese rules about different arrangements in an environment, ranging from buildings to graves. Following those rules will enhance a balance of *yin* ('shady side') and *yang* ('sunny side') and the accumulation of *qi* ('energy') in that environment. Such balance and accumulation of energy will then bring positive effects on the people in that environment or even their future generations. (Mak 2008)

Extract 3

Feng shui is a Chinese system dating to several thousand years ago. The system guides people to design and arrange their homes or workplaces so that *chi* ('energy') can be accumulated to promote the well-being of the people in that environment. To ensure that the system is followed properly, people usually consult some *feng shui* masters when they are about to move into that environment. These masters will advise them on what to do in order to create an environment with the best *feng shui*. (Robins 2000)

Extract 4

Feng shui, an ancient Chinese theory on how to set up a good living or working environment, is exerting its influence on the modern world. It affects not only the interior design of a property but also its market price. While a property with good *feng shui* does not necessarily seek a higher price, one with poor *feng shui*, such as one situated near a graveyard, is less likely to be sold at a high price. (So 2009)

Academic Vocabulary

Describing data and trends

Task 1
Describe data

It should take you fifteen minutes to complete the following tasks. Compare your answers with those of a partner.

A. Put the following phrases in the appropriate column. Add some of your own.

few/little	many	a significant number	the majority
some	a part	a portion	a large number
the minority	a substantial part	sizeable part	ample
a considerable portion	a small part	a slice	a fragment
a segment	an insignificant segment		

B. Match the phrase with the graphic. Suggest one other possible phrase. The first one has been done for you.

| reached a new low | experienced minor fluctuations | held steady |
| fluctuated widely | reached a peak | bottomed out |

1. eventually levelled off

2. _______________________

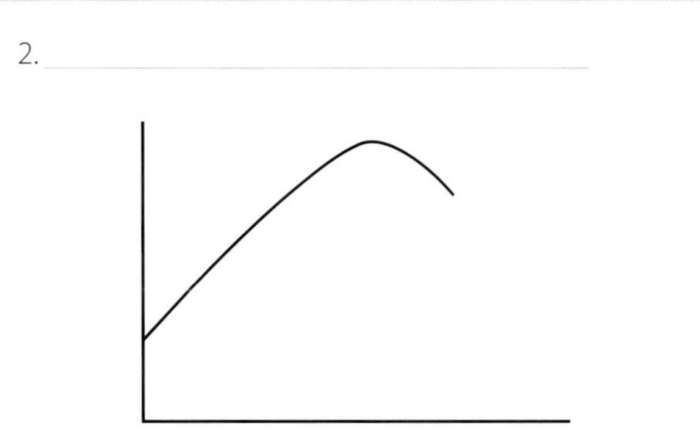

3. _______________________

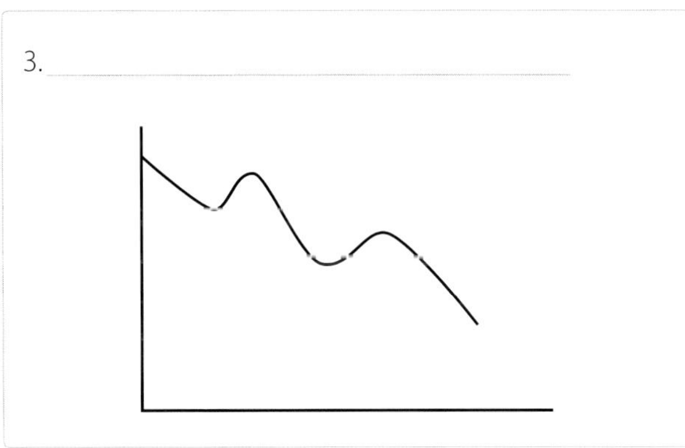

4. _______________________

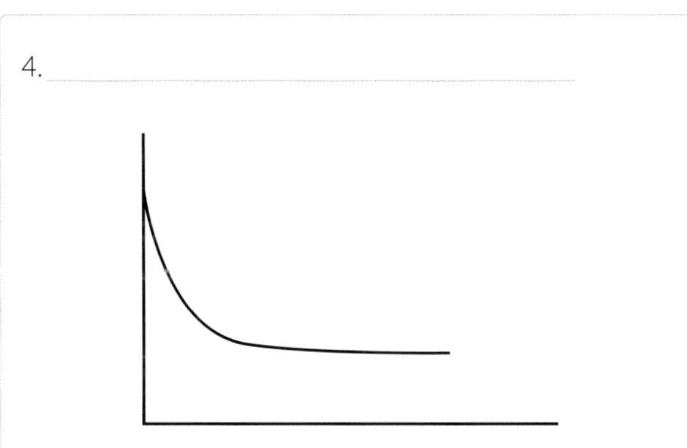

5. _______________________

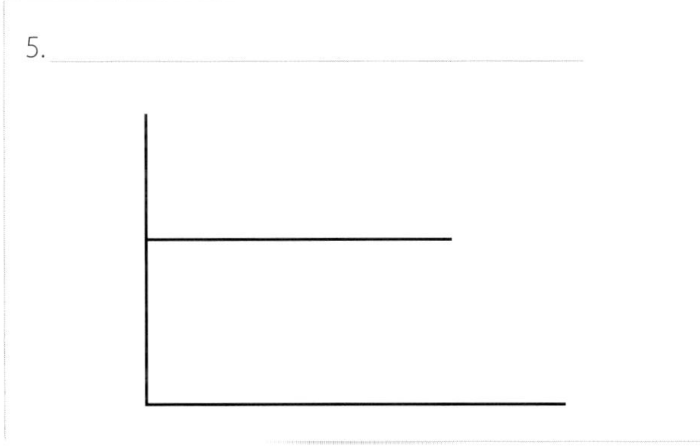

6. _______________________

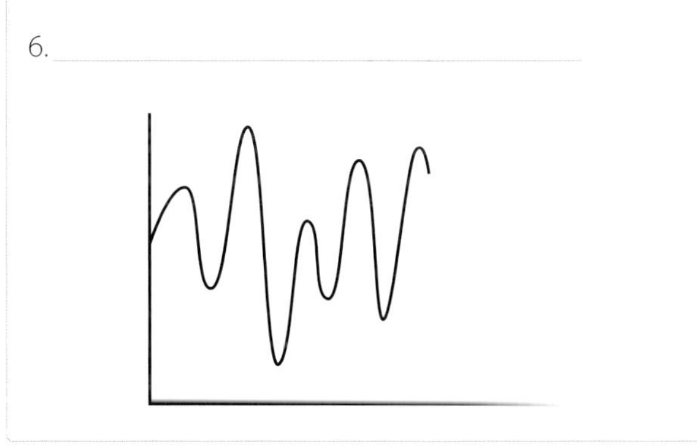

7. _______________________

C. Complete the mind map with as many collocations as you can to describe a trend in data. A few have been done for you.

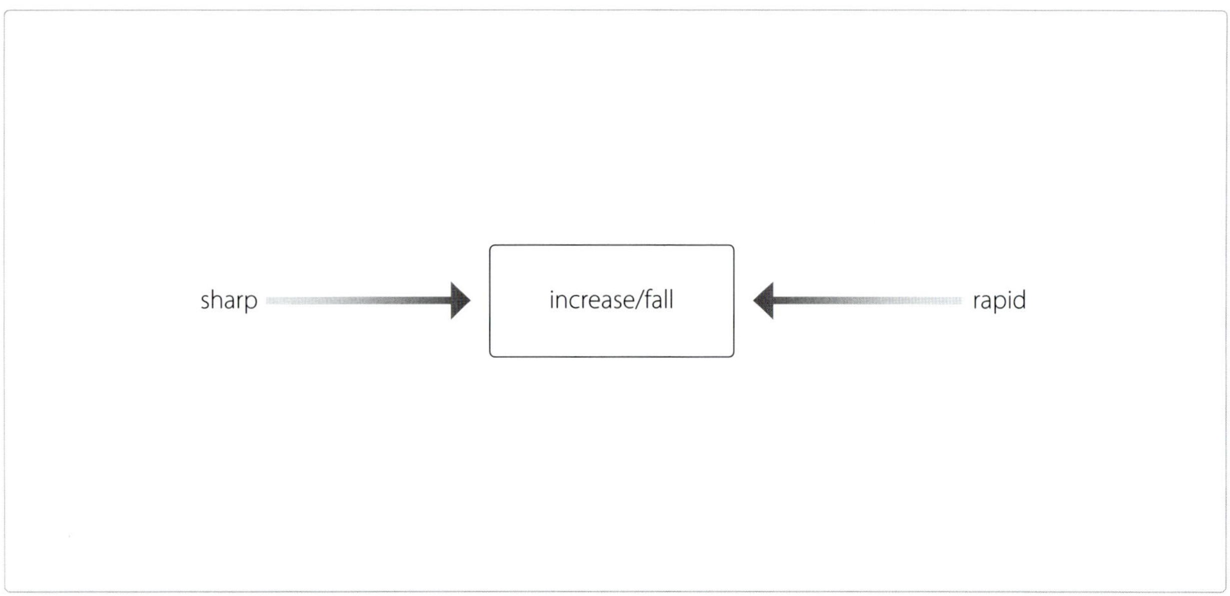

Task 2
Compare and contrast data

Use the sentences with the following phrases to create new sentences. The first one has been done for you as an example. Compare your sentences with those of your partner when you have finished. This should take you ten minutes.

Similar Information	Contrasting Information
both … and …	whereas
similarly	while
in addition	however
also	although
not only … but … also	on the one hand … on the other hand …

1. There were 22 hospital beds per 10,000 population in China in 2005.
   There were 141 hospital beds per 10,000 population in Japan in 2005.

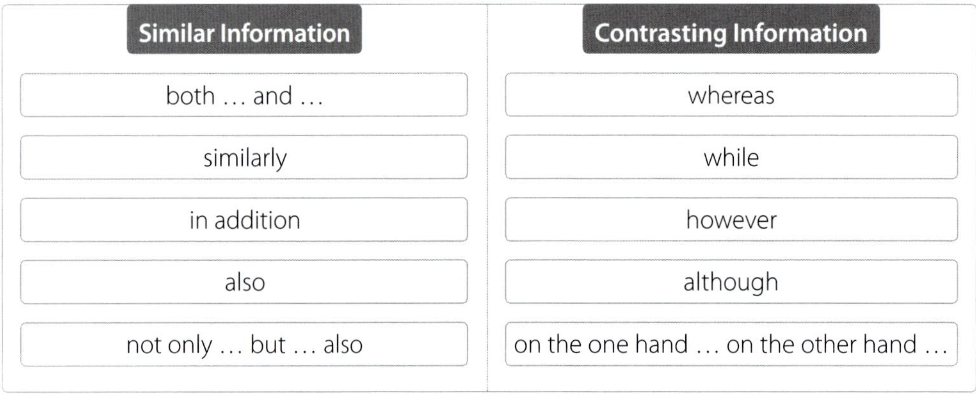

In 2005, there were only 22 hospital beds per 10,000 population in China, whereas there were seven times more hospital beds in Japan (n=141).

2. 36.8% of university-educated Americans did regular exercise in 2000.
   37.6% of university-educated Americans did regular exercise in 2006.

3. The admission rate at colleges and universities in China was 3.6% in 2000.
   The world average university admission rate was 14.3% in 2000.

4. In 2009, 3.1% of Internet users in China were company managers.
   In the same year, 15.0% of Internet users in China were company employees.

5. The unemployment rate for China in 2010 was 4.1%
   The unemployment rate for Hong Kong in 2010 was 4.3%.

Academic Speaking

Describing data and trends

Task 1
Practise describing data and trends

Look at the data below. Do the following:

- Work out what important facts the data are describing.

- Make some notes in the boxes below.

- Practise describing the data with your partner.

Take twenty minutes to do this task.

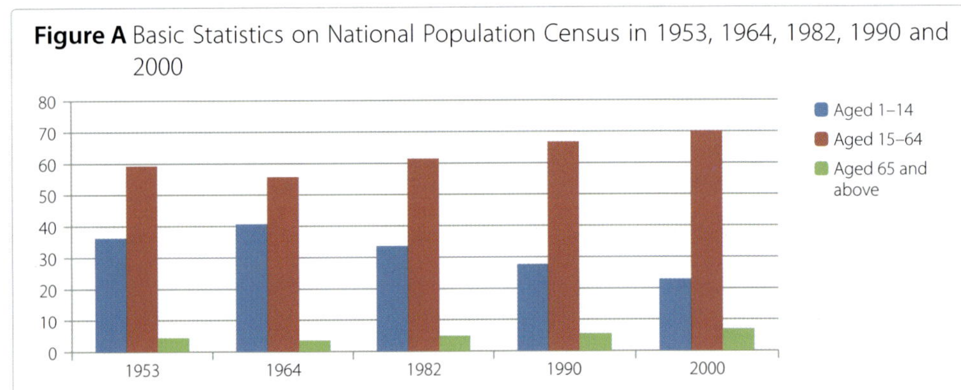

Figure A Basic Statistics on National Population Census in 1953, 1964, 1982, 1990 and 2000

	1953	1964	1982	1990	2000
Ages 1–14	36.28%	40.69%	33.59%	27.69%	22.89%
Ages 15–64	59.31%	55.75%	61.5%	66.74%	70.15%
Ages 65 and over	4.41%	3.56%	4.91%	5.57%	6.96%

(Source: *China Statistical Yearbook 2009*, http://www.stats.gov.cn/tjsj/ndsj/2009/indexeh.htm)

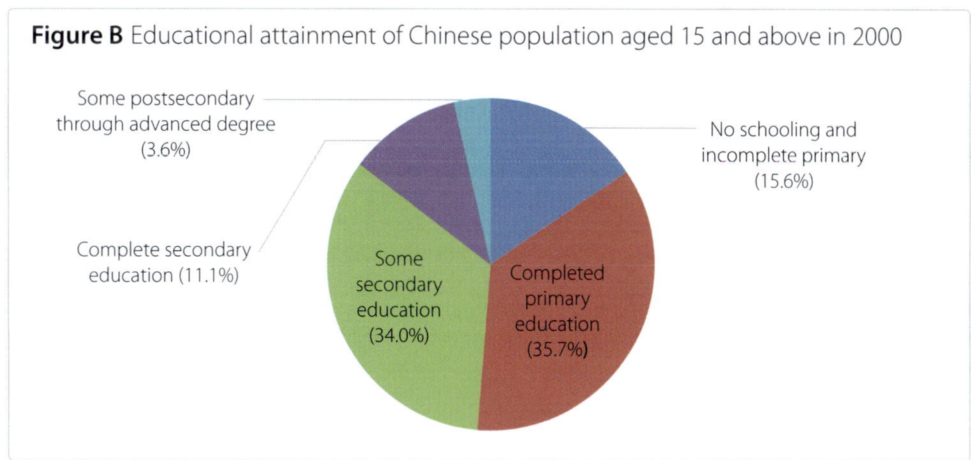

(Pie chart drawn based on information taken from Wikipedia,
http://en.wikipedia.org/wiki/Demographics_of_the_People's_Republic_of_China)

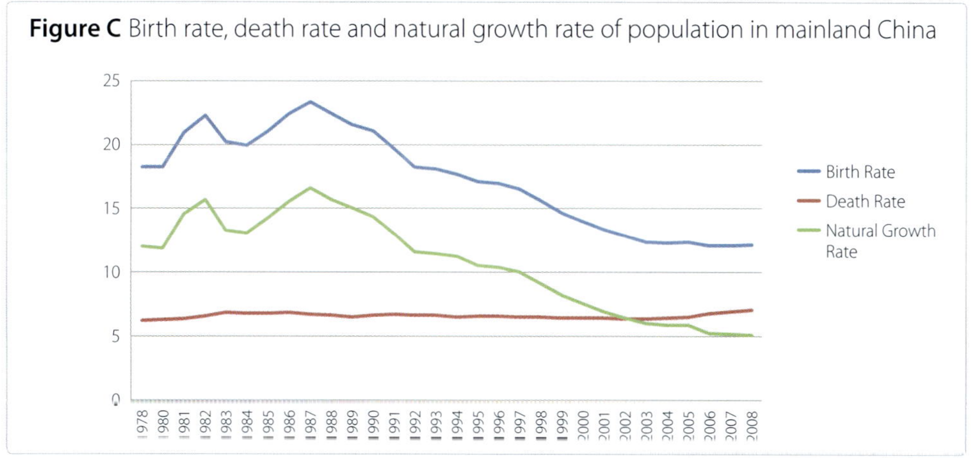

(Line graph drawn according to information in *China Statistical Yearbook 2009*,
http://www.stats.gov.cn/tjsj/ndsj/2009/indexeh.htm)

Academic Speaking Tutorial

Integrating data into a tutorial discussion to support your stance

As we have discussed, data can be an important way to give evidence for your stance. The use of data strengthens your arguments. If people are making claims in tutorial discussions without supporting their stance with evidence, you can ask them for evidence using phrases like the following:

Why do you think that?

What evidence do you have for that?

Are you sure that is true? Why do you think that?

Task 1
Prepare for tutorial discussion

In a moment you are going to have a tutorial discussion about the following topic:

What are some of the problems facing China at the moment? What can be done to solve these problems?

Take fifteen minutes to do the following:

1. Look at the data below.

2. Decide what problems they are highlighting.

3. Make some notes in preparation for the discussion. Use the data below as evidence for your opinions.

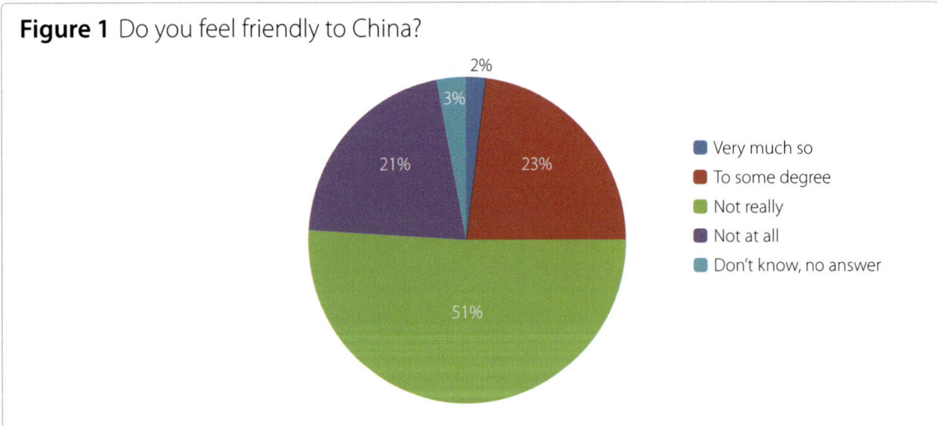

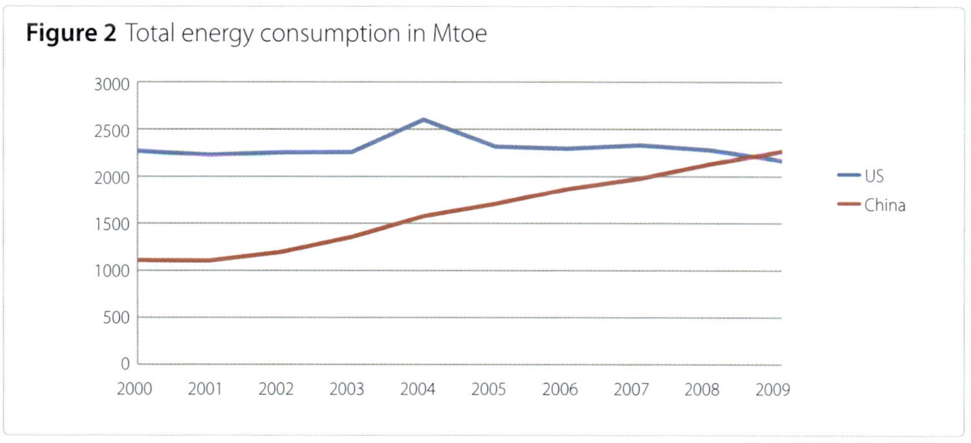

Figure 2 Total energy consumption in Mtoe

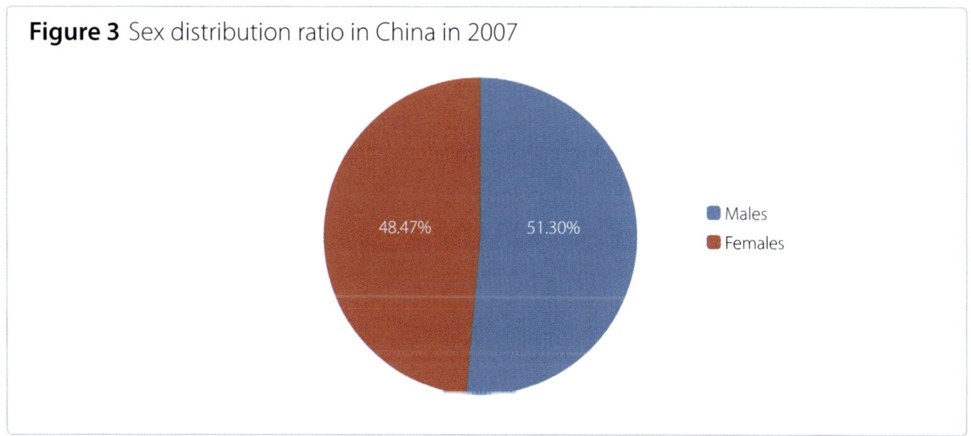

Figure 3 Sex distribution ratio in China in 2007

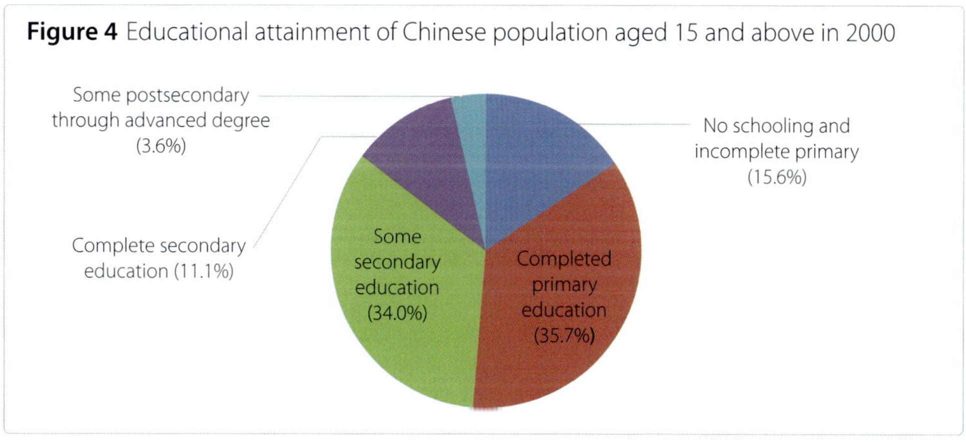

Figure 4 Educational attainment of Chinese population aged 15 and above in 2000

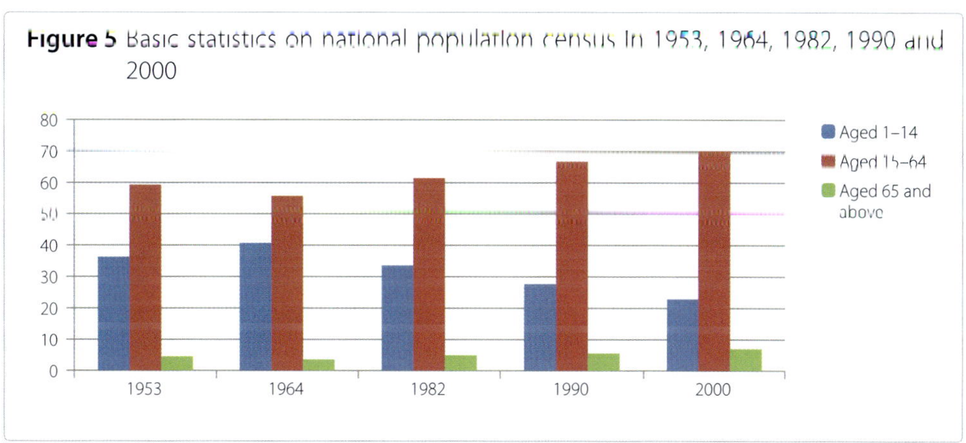

Figure 5 Basic statistics on national population census in 1953, 1964, 1982, 1990 and 2000

Task 1 Prepare for tutorial discussion | Task 2 Participate in a tutorial discussion | Task 3 Analyse your strengths and weaknesses

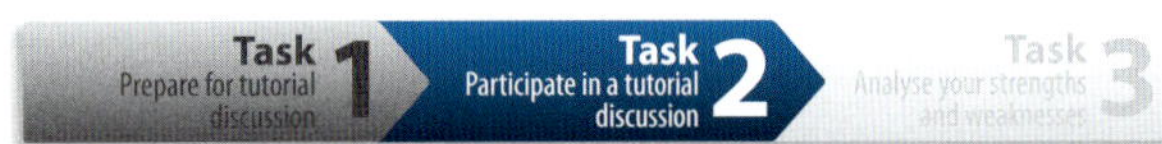

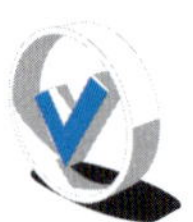

Task 2
Participate in a tutorial discussion

Now, hold a tutorial discussion for thirty minutes. Remember to:

1. use data to support your opinions
2. use citation vocabulary when necessary to strengthen the evidence you use to support your opinions
3. use questions to discuss the issue more deeply
4. agree and disagree when appropriate
5. use the phrases you learned for asking for evidence if other people in your discussion don't use data to support their claims

Task 3
Analyse your strengths and weaknesses

Take five minutes to fill in the form below.

Tutorial Discussion Feedback Form			
I found enough information from my own research to discuss the topic in depth.	☐ Yes	☐ No	☐ Sometimes
The sources of information I found from my own research were all academic sources.	☐ Yes	☐ No	☐ Sometimes
I integrated the information from my reading into the discussion to support my arguments.	☐ Yes	☐ No	☐ Sometimes
My ideas were clearly expressed.	☐ Yes	☐ No	☐ Sometimes
I was able to express myself without frequent hesitations.	☐ Yes	☐ No	☐ Sometimes
I know enough vocabulary to be able to express my thoughts and opinions.	☐ Yes	☐ No	☐ Sometimes
I expressed my agreement with others' ideas.	☐ Yes	☐ No	☐ Sometimes
I expressed my disagreement with others' ideas when necessary and gave reasons.	☐ Yes	☐ No	☐ Sometimes
I helped develop some kind of agreement/consensus when possible.	☐ Yes	☐ No	☐ Sometimes
I helped maintain good group relations by being polite, listening to others, showing understanding and not interrupting.	☐ Yes	☐ No	☐ Sometimes

Ideas for future improvement

Structuring texts for your assignments

Test your knowledge

Answer these questions about Unit 5 with your partner.

1. What kind of information or details do we usually include in the introduction and the conclusion of an essay?

2. What is the function of a summary in a report?

3. What are some common spoken signposts for showing the development of an argument in a tutorial discussion?

Learning outcomes

By the end of this unit, you should be able to:

- structure an essay and a report clearly;
- use linking words and phrases to improve the coherence of a written text; and
- use appropriate signposts in a tutorial discussion.

Now that you have learnt about gathering information for your writing, coming up with your own stance, and synthesizing information into paragraphs, you are ready to construct whole texts. All texts have some kind of structure. The structure of a text depends on the nature of the text, who it is for and what the context is. If a writer doesn't structure a text clearly, it can be difficult for the reader to understand it. As readers, we all have expectations of how texts are going to be structured, and we need to follow these as good writers as well.

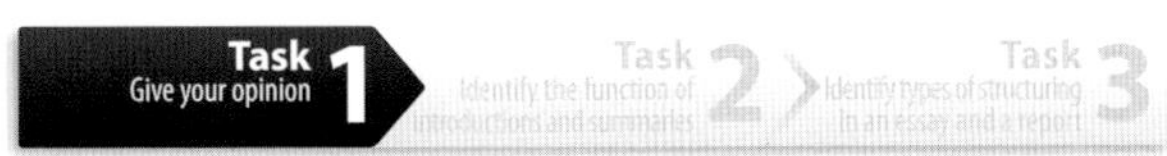

Task 1
Give your opinion

Discuss the following with your partner. Take five minutes to do this.

1. Are you generally happy at the moment?

2. What brings you happiness?

3. How important is it in life to be happy? Are there other things that are more important?

All texts have some kind of structure to them.

Some texts have a more obvious structure than others. For example, a report usually has headings, a numbering system, and even a table of contents if it is a big report. These help to guide the reader through the text. An essay has an introduction which tells the reader the focus and often the structure of the essay. A journal article has an abstract and headings. Even non-academic texts have structure. A novel, for example, has the development of the plot and the characters, which give it structure. The following outlines some ways that academic texts are structured.

1. **Academic texts usually have a section at the beginning of the text which gives the reader an overview of the structure or focus of the text.**

This section at the beginning is different in different academic texts. A journal article has an abstract. Essays have an introduction. Reports have a summary.

Task 2
Identify the function of introductions and summaries

Read the introduction from a student's essay on happiness. Identify the function of each numbered sentence. It should take you ten minutes to do this with your partner.

Introduction from a student essay

1. Over half of all primary school children in Hong Kong say that they are mostly unhappy with their lives (Hawkins 2011). This troubling finding came as a shock to their parents and teachers, who thought that they were trying their best to provide a happy environment for these children. It is findings like these that lead us to question what it is that brings us happiness. 2. The concept of happiness is a complex one and often, whether we feel happy or not depends on which 'level of happiness' we are trying to reach and how we are trying to reach it. 3. Recent psychological research has revealed that we can classify happiness into three levels (Lyubomirsky 2008), which are possession, achievement, and relationship. 4. This essay will discuss them in turn and look at whether any of these alone can bring us a happy and fulfilling life.

Now read a summary from a student's research report on happiness. Identify the function of each numbered sentence. Take another ten minutes to do this with your partner.

Summary from a student report

1. This report aims to examine the happiness level of primary pupils in Hong Kong, in the light of recent suicide cases among children in the territory. 2. One thousand primary pupils in the territory were asked to respond to 20 statements adapted from the Oxford Happiness Questionnaire [1]. These 20 statements fall into the categories of 'meaning of happiness', 'life in general', 'own self', 'family', and 'school'. Results showed that in the eyes of the primary pupils, family, school work, and relationships with classmates are more important sources of happiness than are material gains. 3. Overall, the results indicated that the pupils were found to be not very happy in general. They did not regard themselves as happy people, and they were happy with neither their families nor their school. Their unhappy feelings towards their families and school were believed to be caused by a lack of parental attention and teachers' insufficient attention to them in a large-class learning environment. 4. It is recommended that the family, the school and the government should work together more to enable:

- more parent-children time during which parents can talk to and play with their children;
- small-class teaching and learning at school;
- more funding for the education system; and
- a better work-life balance for parents.

2. The structure of academic texts can be seen in different ways, e.g. in the form of headings, subheadings, a numbering system, topic sentences and linking words.

All of these structuring features help to guide the reader through the text. They tell the reader what to expect. Without these, the reader will feel that something is missing. The reader would have to work a lot harder to understand the text without these structuring features. Above all, academic writing should be clear. Structuring a text and periodically telling the reader about that structure makes the writing clear.

Task 3
Identify types of structuring in an essay and a report

Pair up with someone next to you. Decide who is Student A and Student B. Follow the instructions below. It should take you fifteen minutes to do this.

Student A
Read Text A, student essay. Underline the parts in the text where the writer shows the structure of the text. Look for topic sentences and linking words. Once you have finished, compare your answers with your partner.

Student B
Read Text B, student report. Underline the parts in the text where the writer is showing the reader the structure of the text. Look for headings, a numbering system, links between graphics and text, links between different section and linking words. Once you have finished, compare your answers with your partner.

Text A: Student essay

1   Over half of all primary school children in Hong Kong say that they are mostly unhappy with their lives (Hawkins 2011). This troubling finding came as a shock to their parents and teachers, who thought that they were trying their best to provide a happy environment for these children. It is findings like these that lead us to question what it is that brings us happiness. The concept of happiness is a complex one and often, whether we feel happy or not depends on which 'level of happiness' we are trying to reach and how we are trying to reach it. Recent psychological research has revealed that we can classify happiness into three levels (Lyubomirsky 2008). They are possession, achievement, and relationship. This essay will discuss them in turn and look at whether any of these alone can bring us a happy and fulfilling life.

2   The first level of happiness, the most basic one, is 'possession'. Possession, particularly material possession, brings feelings of happiness (Flynn 2000), and maybe that is why it is also the most direct representation of happiness across generations. To young children, the possession of a toy or a lollipop can bring instant feelings of happiness. When children cry, parents will often wave a toy or a candy in front of their eyes to get their attention and stop them from crying. As the children grow older, the 'toy-or-lollipop trick' does not work anymore but is replaced by different age-appropriate desires, such as a PSP for a teenager or a car for an adult. However, 87% of adults questioned in a survey believed that material possession was not genuine happiness (Hawkins 2011). Increasingly, material desires are seen as a negative influence on happiness even though the object might give us short term feelings of happiness (Richins & Dawson 1992). Once a child finishes a lollipop, he or she will long for another one. An adult, after having checked off an item on the 'desire list', needs to move on to the next material item. In other words, "this type of [material] happiness is strong, but it does not last long" (Sherfield 2004: 83). Therefore, most psychologists believe that we need to move beyond the first level of happiness for a long-term satisfying life.

3   Beyond the first level of happiness is 'achievement', which is not easily measurable. Achievement relates to our success in doing something or demonstrating our ability at something (Aldridge 2005). Educational achievement is what we all are most

familiar with at the early stages of our lives. A student who manages to rank high in an examination can be considered to have achieved something (see Chaplin's [2009] study on different types of achievement as perceived by 300 children and adolescents ages 8–18). Likewise, in the workplace, if a working adult excels at all his or her duties, gains recognition and is given promotion, happiness, again in the form of satisfaction, is felt. This type of happiness tends to last longer than that brought by possession and is therefore at a higher level of the emotional scale.

4   Above the previous two levels of happiness is 'relationship'. Unlike the other two levels, relationship goes beyond one individual and relies on interaction with other people. Relationships come in different forms, such as family bond, friendship, work and marriage (Sherfield 2004). A good relationship with our family members, friends and spouse usually implies a happy social life. For an adult, a close relationship with the spouse/partner leads to feelings of security, self-esteem and happiness (Flynn 2000). These kinds of relationships, at different stages of our lives, lead to longer-lasting happiness than do the other two levels of happiness.

5   From the above, we can see that possession, achievement and relationship constitute three different levels of happiness. These levels all make up much of what it is to be happy. It seems that all are important and that the 'lower' levels will not bring long-term happiness with the high-order levels. However, these emotions are by no means the only important ones in life. It is important to acknowledge that there exist equally important emotions: sadness, anger, desire, love, and worry are all emotions that add richness to life. To be happy all the time would be unnatural, although we would all probably agree that it is worth pursuing happiness.

References

Aldridge, D. (2005). *Case study designs in music therapy*. London; Philadelphia, PA: J. Kingsley Publishers.

Chaplin, L. N. (2009). Please may I have a bike? Better yet, may I have a hug? An examination of children's and adolescents' happiness. *Journal of Happiness Studies* 5: 541–62.

Flynn, E. (2000). *The science of happiness*. Franklin, WI: Sheed & Ward.

Hawkins, A. (2011). The secret to happiness: A report of a wide-scale survey of the level of happiness in Hong Kong. *Journal of Emotions* 63:69–92.

Lyubomirsky, S. (2008). *The how of happiness: A scientific approach to getting the life you want*. New York: Penguin Press.

Richins, M. L. & S. Dawson (1992). A consumer values orientation for materialism and its measurement: Scale development and validation. *Journal of Consumer Research* 19: 303–16.

Sherfield, R. M. (2004). *The everything self-esteem book: Boost your confidence, achieve inner strength, and learn to love yourself*. Avon, MA: Adams Media.

Text B: Student report
(Some parts of the report have been taken out to reduce reading time.)

A survey on the happiness level of primary pupils in Hong Kong

Summary

This report aims to examine the happiness level of primary pupils in Hong Kong, in the light of recent suicide cases among children in the territory. One thousand primary pupils in the territory were asked to respond to 20 statements adapted from the Oxford Happiness Questionnaire [1]. These 20 statements fall into the categories of 'meaning of happiness', 'life in general', 'own self', 'family', and 'school'. Results showed that in the eyes of the primary pupils, family, school work, and relationships with classmates are more important sources of happiness than material gains. Overall, the results indicated that the pupils were found to be not very happy in general. They did not regard themselves as happy people, and they were happy with neither their families nor their school. Their unhappy feelings towards their families and school were believed to be caused by a lack of parental attention and teachers' insufficient attention to them in a large-class learning environment.

It is recommended that the family, the school and the government should work together more to enable:

1. more parent–children time during which parents can talk to and play with their children;

2. small-class teaching and learning at school;

3. more funding for the education system; and

4. a better work–life balance for parents.

1. Background

The recent suicides of two primary pupils in Tai Po within two weeks have stimulated much discussion about the mental health and development of Hong Kong primary pupils in society. Of particular concern is whether pupils, being so young, are enjoying their lives, and this is the focus of the survey presented in this report. The purpose of the study is to investigate what happiness means to a group of primary pupils and whether they are happy with their lives.

2. Existing studies on happiness

…

3. Methodology

A total of 20 statements, adapted from the Oxford Happiness Questionnaire [1], were presented to 1,000 local primary pupils. These 20 questions fell into five groups: *meaning of happiness*, *life in general*, *own self*, *family*, and *school*. The pupils were asked to rate the statements in each group according to a scale of 1 (strongly disagree) to 4 (strongly agree). The statements were presented to the pupils in Chinese, their mother tongue, so that they could understand them. The research team went over the statements with the pupils and answered any queries before they started and while they were responding to the statements.

The data collected were analysed according to each group (e.g. *life in general*) and each statement (e.g. statement 5: *Being alive is good*). The average of all statements for each rating was treated as the overall rating of the particular group concerned. The results are described in Section 4, and the implication of these results is discussed in Section 5. Recommendations are made in Section 6.

4. Results and findings

The ratings of the five groups of items and the analysis are listed below:

4.1. *Group 1: Meaning of happiness*

The survey started with four possible sources of happiness in the daily lives of primary schools: material gains, school work, family and classmates/friends. The ratings for these sources are listed in Table 1.

Table 1: Sources of happiness

Items: I am happy when I …	Number of pupils for each rating				Average ratings
	1 ·········· 2 ·········· 3 ·········· 4				
	(Strongly disagree)			(Strongly agree)	
1. have a lot of pocket money/ toys/PSPs	12	235	550	203	2.9
2. get good results at school	20	65	405	510	3.4
3. am with my parents	10	33	312	645	3.6
4. am with my classmates/ friends	58	156	245	541	3.3

All four items scored high on the positive ratings ('3' and '4'). Good school results, parents and classmates/friends scored the highest in rating '4', whereas material gain such as pocket money and toys scored rating '3'. These ratings reveal that all four sources were important in the eyes of the primary pupils, and parents, friends and school results are more essential than is material gain.

4.2. Group 2: Life in general

Table 2 presents the ratings of the four items among the primary pupils.

Table 2: Life in general

Items	Number of pupils for each rating				Average ratings
	1 ·········· 2 ·········· 3 ·········· 4				
	(No)			(Yes)	
5. Being alive is good.	115	535	250	100	2.3
6. My life is full of hope.	153	436	301	110	2.4
7. My life is happy.	324	476	102	98	2
8. The world is a good place to live in.	260	275	235	230	2.4

Unlike the rather positive picture shown in Table 1, Table 2 reveals a rather disturbing picture of what the young participants thought about their lives. All four aspects on 'life in general' scored the highest in rating, '2', resulting in an average rating nearer to the negative side on the scale (1' and '2'). Of the four aspects, 'my life is happy' had the lowest rating on average, implying discontent among the participating pupils with the lives they were leading. It is worrying to see that they held a negative or pessimistic view even at such a young age.

4.3. Group 3: Own self

…

4.4. Group 4: Family

…

4.5. Group 5: School

…

5. Discussion
The negative views of the pupils towards their lives, as revealed in the above analysis, can be interpreted in the following areas:

…

6. Conclusions and recommendations
Worryingly, this study has found that the participating primary pupils are not happy and are not enjoying their lives. On the whole, they are not happy with their family life or their school life; that might be why they held a negative view towards their own lives. Their unhappiness with their families might be due to a lack of communication between them and their parents. Most of the parents work long hours and have little time to spend with their children. At school, the problem that the pupils faced seems to be related to the large class size in which they had little attention from their teachers.

In light of the above, there is an urgent need to find ways to create a happier environment for the young generation. Both parents and schools, in particular, should take action, because school and the home are the two most influential environments for young children. There are no easy solutions, as the situation is caused by the particular social and economic environment of Hong Kong. We all know that parents should allocate as much time as possible to nurture their children. However, this is difficult when employers expect long working hours from their employees. Schools should have smaller teacher-student ratios so that teachers can give more attention to students. However, reducing teacher-student ratios is also difficult to achieve when schools are hindered from doing this because of a lack of government funding. It is likely that if positive change happens, it will only happen when governments make work–life balance a priority and set guidelines on maximum working hours and put more funding into the education system. The government has to understand that it is worth investing in the happiness of their future voters.

References

[1] Hills, P. & M. Argyle, M. (2002). The Oxford Happiness Questionnaire: A compact scale for the measurement of psychological well-being. *Personality and Individual Differences* 33: 1073–82.

Homework
Apply skills to another course

Write an analysis of the structure of a text from one of your courses. Explain the following:

- what type of text it is

- how it is structured

- what examples of the language are used to show the structure

Do this in less than 300 words.

Evaluating ideas and data in a text

Task 1
Read for understanding, and give your opinion

Look at the student report and the student essay on happiness. Read the text you haven't read. Then answer the following questions. Compare your answers with those of the person next to you. It should take you twenty minutes to do this task.

1. What are the three levels of happiness mentioned in the essay?

2. What do you think of this categorization?

3. How is happiness evaluated in the report? Do you think this is a logical method?

4. How happy are primary school students? What data support this?

5. Do you agree with the recommendations made in the report and with the conclusion in the essay? If not, what changes would you have made?

Academic Grammar

Using linking words and phrases

Task 1
Order sentences

The following sentences are from a paragraph, but they are in the wrong order. Put them in the correct order. When you have finished, tell your partner how you worked out the order.

This should take you five minutes. The first one has been done for you.

1. The solutions to these problems are difficult to determine.

2. As a result, there are fewer employment opportunities for people when they reach adulthood.

3. Poverty is a serious problem in the developing world and causes many problems.

4. However, a lack of access to medical care is also a serious concern.

5. For example, without money, children cannot gain a high level of education.

6. In fact, this is the cause of the low life-expectancy rates in many countries in Africa.

7. Likewise, many parts of Asia such as Cambodia and Burma have this problem.

3 > ☐ > ☐ > ☐ > ☐ > ☐ > ☐

Linking words and phrases

In academic writing, there are different words and phrases that are used to link ideas and sentences to show their relationship. These are common in academic writing in explaining complex ideas with complex cause-effect relationships.

The following are the most common types of linking words and phrases used in academic writing:

1. Addition: *moreover, besides this, furthermore, in addition, what is more*

e.g. Having a positive attitude will do you good. **Besides this**, it will affect the people around you in a positive manner.

2. Similarity: *similarly, on a similar basis, likewise, in the same way*

e.g. This achievement will bring happiness, in the form of satisfaction, to not only the student but also the parents. **Likewise**, in the workplace, if a working adult finishes all his/her duties, gains recognition and is given a promotion, happiness, again in the form of satisfaction, ensues.

3. Opposite or Contrast: *however, on the other hand, in contrast, on the contrary, nevertheless* e.g. Possession of what is desired brings a good feeling—happiness. **However**, tangible or material possession is not genuine happiness.

4. Result: *as a result, hence, thus, therefore, as a consequence, consequently, accordingly*

e.g. Some people take everything for granted and never treasure what they possess. **As a result**, no matter what and how much they have, they never feel happy.

5. Exemplification: *for example, for instance*

e.g. Happiness comes in different forms. **For example**, when we have received a gift, we feel happy; when we have achieved something, we also feel happy.

6. Emphasis: *in fact, as a matter of fact*

e.g. People who are not content with what they have do not feel happy. **In fact**, they will never be happy.

7. Sequence or order: *first(ly), second(ly), third(ly), next, last(ly), then*

e.g. There are two basic steps we can follow to develop a positive attitude. **First**, we should understand what we can and cannot change. **Next**, we need to appreciate what we have already possessed or achieved.

Task 2
Identify linking words and phrases

Identify the linking words and phrases in the text and their function (e.g. addition, contrast). The first one has been done for you. Take ten minutes to do this task.

The first level of happiness, the most basic one, is 'possession'. Possession, particularly material possession, brings feelings of happiness (Flynn 2000), <u>and</u> maybe that is why it is also the most direct representation of happiness across generations. To young children, the possession of a toy or a lollipop can bring instant feelings of happiness. When children cry, parents will often wave a toy or a candy in front of their eyes to get their attention and stop them from crying. As the children grow older, the 'toy-or-lollipop trick' does not work anymore but is replaced by different age-appropriate desires, such as a PSP for a teenager or a car for an adult. However, 87% of adults questioned in a survey believed that material possession is not genuine happiness (Hawkins 2011). Increasingly, material desires are seen as a negative influence on happiness even though the object might give us short-term feelings of happiness (Richins & Dawson 1992). Once a child finishes a lollipop, he or she will long for another one. An adult, after having checked off an item on the 'desire list', needs to move on to the next material item. In other words, "this type of [material] happiness is strong, but it does not last long" (Sherfield 2004: 83). Therefore, most psychologists believe that we need to move beyond the first level of happiness for a long-term satisfying life.

<table>
<tr><td>Linking word/phrase</td><td colspan="2">Type</td></tr>
<tr><td>1. and</td><td>addition</td><td></td></tr>
<tr><td>2.</td><td></td><td></td></tr>
<tr><td>3.</td><td></td><td></td></tr>
</table>

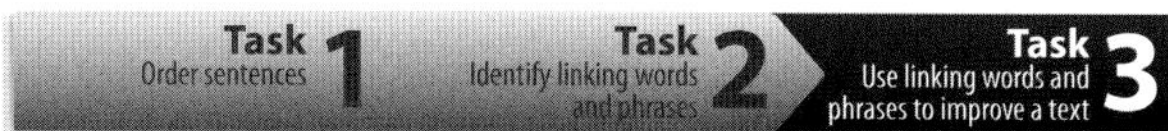

Task 3
Use linking words and phrases to improve a text

Insert some linking words and phrases in the text below. Make any other changes you want to in order to make the text more coherent. This task should take you ten minutes.

The life of a perfectionist is less happy than that of an optimist. Perfectionists will only feel contented when they have accomplished a goal. The process of accomplishing the goal is never important to them; only the outcome is. They move on to the next goal once they have attained a goal. This is a never-ending process. If one goal is not achieved, they easily feel depressed. They don't know how to fail and learn from the experience. Optimists pay attention to both the goal and the process. Optimists set high goals for themselves. They may change their approach to achieve their goal if there is any change in the environment. Even if they cannot achieve the goal, they will look for anything positive that that they can learn from the experience. They can treat criticism from people as some kind of feedback that they can learn from. They are more forgiving and tend to lead a happier life than perfectionists.

Reference

Ben-Shahar, T. (2011). *Being happy: You don't have to be perfect to lead a richer, happier life.* New York: McGraw Hill.

 ## Writing a well-structured text

Introductions and conclusions in academic essays

All academic essays should have an introduction, body paragraphs and a conclusion. The introduction and conclusion are two crucial structural signposts in the essay. They tell the reader the focus and main ideas of the essay.

Introduction

Do not underestimate the importance of your introduction, as it is the readers' gateway to your writing. An introduction **usually** includes the following components:

- **Attention grabbers.** These are strategies used to create interest. Examples include items such as (1) stirring statistics, (2) a quote from an expert, (3) current news and issues, (4) analogy, and (5) facts. Try to stay away from questions directly addressing the reader. Students often write these in the wrong tone, and the questions themselves tend to be too general and not very interesting.

- **Background information.** This will help the readers gain an insight into the topic. You can do this by introducing the wider issues and gradually narrowing them down to your focus.

- **Writer's stance.** As discussed, this is a sentence which captures the essence and key thoughts of an essay. By locating this sentence, a reader should be able to understand your stance.

- **Definitions (optional).** Incorporate the explanations of technical terms which might not be easily understood by readers. Because it is not obligatory to provide definitions in the introduction, do so only when necessary.

- **Overview of the essay.** Giving an overview will help readers understand the scope of the text and follow your argument through the essay. The overview is usually placed at the end of the introduction, after the stance.

Conclusion

A conclusion brings together the whole essay. It helps reinforce the key ideas. It **usually** consists of the following components:

- **Restatement of the stance**. After presenting all your arguments in the body paragraphs, remind your reader what your stance is.

- **Summary of key points**. Remind your readers of the arguments for this stance by summarizing your key points.

- **Looking to the future**. A common way to end an essay is to look to the future by making **recommendations or predictions**; for example, recommendations for the government, for further research on the topic, or how the situation you are talking about might change.

Important: Avoid adding any new ideas in this section. This should be a conclusion and not another paragraph for new information.

Task 1
Write an introduction and a conclusion

Imagine that you have to write an essay on the following topic:

> Every financial year, the Hong Kong Government has to decide who to allocate money and resources to. It is difficult to decide which groups of people are the most in need of support. Decisions such as these are based on political, ethical, and social considerations. Write an essay outlining the three categories of people you think are the most in need in Hong Kong, what support they need and why.

Look at the following essay plan. Use this to write an introduction and a conclusion for the essay. Take twenty minutes to do this task. When you have finished, compare your writing with that of your partner.

Introduction

Paragraph 1—Hong Kong people living beneath the poverty line

Poverty = people living on a monthly income less than or equal to half of the median income of the average household, e.g. less than $3,000 a month in 2005

14.8% in 1995 rising to 17.66% in 2005

Need government employment initiatives

Need education training programmes for undereducated people

Need a transport support scheme to aid travels costs for people in rural areas

Paragraph 2—Domestic Helpers

In 2010, 284,901 domestic helpers in Hong Kong

Important contribution to the economy; without them many families would not be able to have two incomes

Many arrive in serious debt to employment agencies; many take out loans from loan sharks

Also makes them reluctant to report abuse when paid below the minimum wage or forced to work without a rest day

Need protection from being forced to pay high fees to employment agencies, which places them in debt

Need free legal advice

Paragraph 3—Migrants from the mainland

Recent cases of suicide of mainland migrants; one case of mother who threw her children off the 24th floor of apartment building and then jumped to her death

Certain number of women abandoned by Hong Kong husbands

Feel isolated

Limited employment opportunities

Need language classes

Need access to low-rent housing

Need quicker access to welfare in desperate cases

Conclusion

Task 2
Plan the structure of a report

Write an outline for a report on an OHT on the following topic:

> Collect some qualitative and quantitative data on the values that a range of university students hold. Write a report which outlines the methodology, the results, and the significance of the findings.

Think about the following:

1. What will be the heading for each major section?

2. What will be the subheadings?

3. What kind of numbering system will you use?

4. What kind of graphics will you use? Where will you put them?

Be ready to show the rest of the class your ideas. It should take you twenty minutes to do this.

Homework
Preparation for the speaking tutorial

You will discuss the following topic in the speaking tutorial next week:

Every financial year, the Hong Kong Government has to decide who to allocate money and resources to. It is difficult to decide which groups of people are the most in need of support. Which three categories of people do you think are the most in need in Hong Kong? What support do they need the most?

For homework, search for information on this topic. Read it and decide on your stance. Bring evidence to the speaking tutorial to support your stance in the form of ideas and data from your reading.

Academic Vocabulary

Signposting in tutorial discussions

We have talked about how written texts are structured using signposts. Signposts can also help make your speaking more coherent.

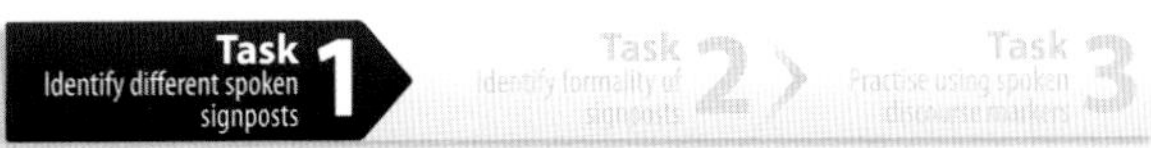

Task 1
Identify different spoken signposts

Read the examples of different types of signposts. Add three examples of your own for each type. Complete this task with the person next to you. It should take you ten minutes to do this.

Signposts for providing specific examples and evidence

To be more specific, …

For example …

Signposts for expressing personal views

Personally, I think …

As far as I know, …

I believe that …

Signposts for expressing doubt
I'm not sure if …
I'm not convinced that …

Signposts for expressing support
That's a good point …
I couldn't agree with you more …
You took the words right out of my mouth …

Signposts for keeping the discussion on topic
What we should be discussing is …
I don't think that is really relevant …

Task 2
Identify formality of signposts

Look at the signposts you have written down. Answer the following questions with your partner.

1. Which signposts are more formal?

2. Which signposts are less formal?

It should take you five minutes to do this task.

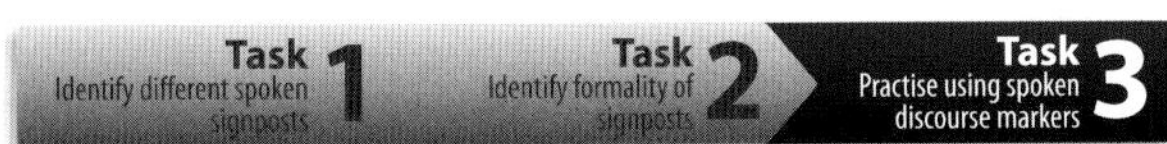

Task 3
Practise using spoken discourse markers

Work in pairs. Turn to your partner and debate one of the following statements for five minutes. Try to use some of the signposts from the task above.

It is better to wait until you are older to start a family.

Living on your own brings more happiness than unhappiness.

Academic Speaking

Responding to opposing arguments

Arguments and opposing arguments in tutorial discussions

When preparing for a tutorial discussion, it is important to think about your own opinion. It is **also** important to think about what people are likely to say, who will disagree with you, and what your response will be to those arguments.

If you do this, you will have a stronger and clearer argument. Thinking about the opposing argument to your own will help you to strengthen your own case.

The following are some expressions that speakers use to exchange opinions.

Asking for opinions

> – What are your views on this topic?

> – Do you agree?

Presenting your own opinion

> – Well, I think …

> – It seems to me that …

> – In my view …

Responding to opposing arguments

> – I take your point, but …

> – I understand what you're saying, but …

> – Well, I'm not sure if that's quite true …

> – But surely …

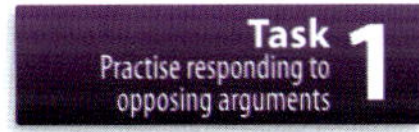

Task 1
Practise responding to opposing arguments

Look at the two statements below.

> Statement 1: Free health care should not be given to smokers

> Statement 2: Advertising of junk food should be banned

Pair up with the person next to you. Take one of the following roles:

Student A: You agree with statements 1 and 2. Make some notes in the box below about why you agree. Your partner will disagree with the two statements. Anticipate what arguments he or she is likely to make. Prepare your response.

Student B: You disagree with statements 1 and 2. Make some notes in the box below about why you disagree. Your partner will agree with the two statements. Anticipate what arguments he or she is likely to make. Prepare your response.

Now, take ten minutes to discuss Statement 1. Your challenge is to see if you can continue to discuss the topic without stopping, all the time responding to the opposing arguments of your partner.

When you have finished, spend ten minutes discussing Statement 2.

This whole task should take you thirty minutes.

Academic Speaking Tutorial

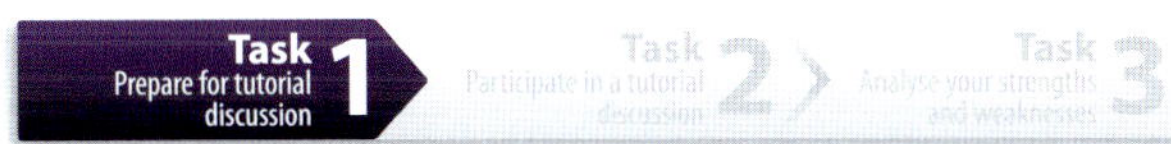

Task 1
Prepare for tutorial discussion

In a moment you are going to have a tutorial discussion about the following topic:

> Every financial year, the Hong Kong Government has to decide who to allocate money and resources to. It is difficult to decide which groups of people are the most in need of support. Which three categories of people do you think are the most in need in Hong Kong? What support do they need the most?

Take fifteen minutes to transfer the notes that you took for homework into the following table.

	Your stance	Evidence
Which types of people need the most funding from the government?		
What support do they need?		

Task 2
Participate in a tutorial discussion

Now, hold a tutorial discussion for thirty minutes. Remember to:

1. use evidence from the texts you brought to support your opinions

2. use citation vocabulary when necessary, to strengthen the evidence you use to support your opinions

3. use signalling phrases to structure what you are saying, to make it clear to your audience

4. use questions to stimulate deeper discussion

5. agree and disagree when appropriate

6. use the phrases for asking for evidence if other people in your discussion don't use data to support their claims

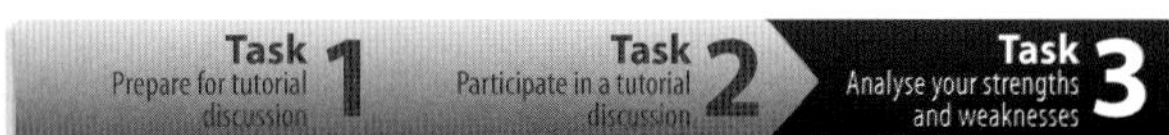

Task 3
Analyse your strengths and weaknesses

Take five minutes to fill in the form below.

Tutorial Discussion Feedback Form			
I found enough information from my own research to discuss the topic in depth.	☐ Yes	☐ No	☐ Sometimes
The sources of information I found from my own research were all academic sources of information.	☐ Yes	☐ No	☐ Sometimes
I integrated the information from my reading into the discussion to support my arguments.	☐ Yes	☐ No	☐ Sometimes
My ideas were clearly expressed.	☐ Yes	☐ No	☐ Sometimes
I was able to express myself without frequent hesitations.	☐ Yes	☐ No	☐ Sometimes
I know enough vocabulary to be able to express my thoughts and opinions.	☐ Yes	☐ No	☐ Sometimes
I expressed my agreement with others' ideas.	☐ Yes	☐ No	☐ Sometimes
I expressed my disagreement with others' ideas when necessary and gave reasons.	☐ Yes	☐ No	☐ Sometimes
I helped develop some kind of agreement/consensus when possible.	☐ Yes	☐ No	☐ Sometimes
I helped maintain good group relations by being polite, listening to others, showing understanding and not interrupting.	☐ Yes	☐ No	☐ Sometimes

Ideas for future improvement

Homework
Apply skills to another course

Bring in the following to the next lesson in hardcopy:

- an essay or a report you have written for a course this semester (it should be a full text, written to a standard that you would be happy handing in)

- a copy of the assignment topic and any guidelines you have been given such as how it should be structured, the word limit, etc.

Editing your written assignments

Test your knowledge

Answer these questions about Unit 6 with your partner.

1. How important is it to edit your written assignments?

2. What are the best strategies for editing?

3. What are some common problems with a text which require editing?

Learning outcomes

By the end of this unit, you should be able to:

- identify aspects of a written text that need editing;

- proofread a text and identify some grammatical errors; and

- rewrite part of an academic text in order to improve it.

Overview of Unit

The final stage of the writing process is editing. Writers tend to underestimate the time and effort it takes to edit a text into a good final product. This is certainly the case for most students. Most of them leave writing too late to do enough editing. In this unit we will look at strategies that you can use to produce a better final text. We will review a lot of what we have talked about in this textbook in order to do this.

The editing process

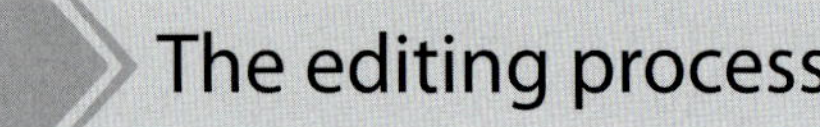

Task 1
Discuss different views of the writing process

Read the following quotes from famous writers. Discuss what these tell us about writing and the editing process. Take ten minutes to do this with your partner.

Quotes

- I'm not a very good writer, but I'm an excellent rewriter. —James Michener
- The wastebasket is a writer's best friend. —Isaac Bashevis Singer
- The best style is the style you don't notice. —Somerset Maugham
- Sleep on your writing; take a walk over it; scrutinize it of a morning; review it of an afternoon; digest it after a meal; let it sleep in your drawer a twelvemonth; never venture a whisper about it to your friend, if he be an author especially. —A. Bronson Alcott
- Every writer I know has trouble writing. —Joseph Heller
- When something can be read without effort, great effort has gone into its writing. —Enrique Jardiel Poncela
- Easy reading is damn hard writing. —Nathaniel Hawthorne

(Source: http://www.quotegarden.com/writing.html)

Getting someone to read your assignment and give feedback

One of the best ways to start the editing process is to get someone to read your assignment. You should always write with the reader in mind and try to make sure that the assignment is clear and understandable.

When something can be read without effort, great effort has gone into its writing.

—Enrique Jardiel Poncela

The best way to check that you have made yourself clear to your reader is to test this by getting someone to read it.

It is important to choose someone appropriate, however, to read your text. You should choose someone who has some knowledge of the area you have written about. The person doesn't have to be an expert but has to be able to understand the basic ideas you are talking about and the terminology that you are using. Someone taking the same course as you would be a good choice. You can pair up and do this for each other.

Criteria for assessing a written assignment

In this textbook, we have looked at four stages of the writing process. In each of these stages we have looked at different skills you need to be able to complete a well-written academic assignment. We can turn these skills into questions for the reader who is helping to edit the text. These are outlined in the table below.

Unit	Focus of the Unit	Questions for the reader
2	Gathering information for your assignments	• Have I analysed the assignment question correctly? • Have I referred to good academic texts in my assignment? (Look at the reference list.) • Have I chosen texts which allow me to discuss the complexities of the assignment topic? • Have I rewritten the ideas of others into my own words and not relied too heavily on quotations?
3	Finding and expressing your stance for your assignments	• Is my stance on the assignment topic clear? • Has my stance been supported enough with evidence from my reading? • Is the evidence I have used convincing?
4	Synthesizing your own and others' ideas for your assignments	• Have I combined my stance and the evidence into clear and logical paragraphs (essays)/sections (reports)? • Are there good topic sentences (essays)/headings (reports) for each part of the assignment?
5	Structuring texts for your assignments	• Does the text have a clear and logical structure? • Is there an appropriate introduction (essays)/summary (reports) at the beginning and a conclusion at the end? • Is it easy to understand the development of ideas throughout the text through the use of linking words and phrases?

Of course, you should also ask yourself these questions. The following is a checklist that you can use. There is space for you and a reader to assess the text.

Task 2

Analyse the weaknesses of a written assignment

Work with a partner. Swap your written assignment and assignment guidelines with your partner. Read each other's work and fill in the checklist below. It should take you thirty minutes to do this task.

	Questions	You		Reader	
Supporting information	Has the assignment question been analysed correctly?	☐ Yes	☐ No	☐ Yes	☐ No
	Have I referred to good academic texts in my assignment? (Look at the reference list.)	☐ Yes	☐ No	☐ Yes	☐ No
	Have I chosen texts which allow me to discuss the complexities of the assignment topic?	☐ Yes	☐ No	☐ Yes	☐ No
	Have I rewritten the ideas of others into my own words and not relied too heavily on quotations?	☐ Yes	☐ No	☐ Yes	☐ No
Stance	Is my stance on the assignment topic clear?	☐ Yes	☐ No	☐ Yes	☐ No
	Has my stance been supported enough with evidence from my reading?	☐ Yes	☐ No	☐ Yes	☐ No
	Is the evidence I have used convincing?	☐ Yes	☐ No	☐ Yes	☐ No
Synthesizing	Have I combined my stance and the evidence into clear and logical paragraphs (essays)/sections (reports)?	☐ Yes	☐ No	☐ Yes	☐ No
	Are there good topic sentences (essays)/headings (reports) for each part of the assignment?	☐ Yes	☐ No	☐ Yes	☐ No
Structuring	Does the text have a clear and logical structure?	☐ Yes	☐ No	☐ Yes	☐ No
	Is there an appropriate introduction (essays)/summary (reports) at the beginning and a conclusion at the end?	☐ Yes	☐ No	☐ Yes	☐ No
	Is it easy to understand the development of ideas throughout the text through the use of linking words and phrases?	☐ Yes	☐ No	☐ Yes	☐ No

Other Comments

Once you have got a reader to give you feedback, and you have assessed the text yourself, you need to decide what you need to do to improve it. The following are some areas that you might need to work on.

- making the writing more concise because it is over the word limit

- adding evidence to support your stance

- working on the paragraphing

- working on the structuring of the text as a whole

- working on the grammatical accuracy

Academic Writing

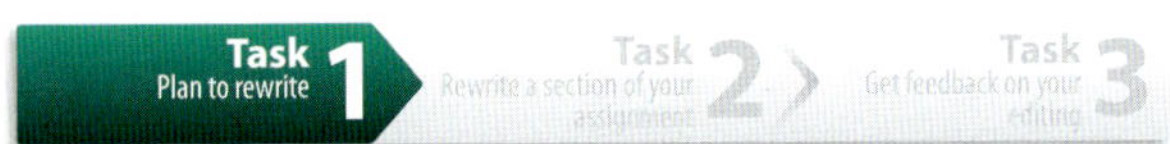

Task 1
Plan to rewrite

Look at the feedback you received on your assignment. Identify one section of your text that you should rewrite. You should be able to rewrite it in thirty minutes, so it shouldn't be the whole text. It could be the introduction and the first paragraph of an essay. It could be the headings and the numbering system of a report. Before you do this, however, make some notes below about what you need to change. This should take you ten minutes.

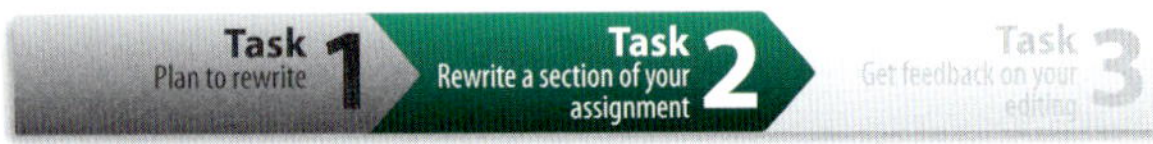

Task 2
Rewrite a section of your assignment

Now spend the next thirty minutes rewriting that section of your assignment.

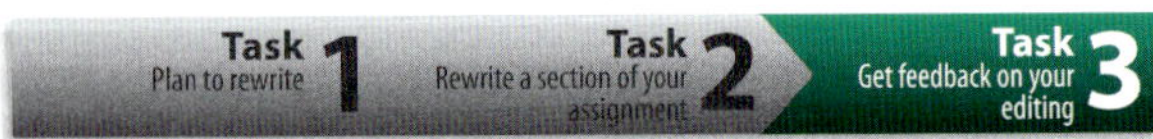

Task 3
Get feedback on your editing

Show your edited draft to the same person who read your assignment at the beginning of the lesson. Explain what you have changed. Get feedback on whether the changes have improved the text or not. It should take you a further twenty minutes to do this task.

Academic Grammar

Proofreading

Task 1
Proofread your written assignment

In Unit 1, we looked at eight common areas of grammatical weakness for university students in Hong Kong. They are:

1. **countable/uncountable nouns**

2. **articles** (a/an/the is wrong, missing, or redundant)

3. **prepositions** (wrong, missing, or redundant)

4. **active/passive voice**

5. **participles**, present participle **~ing**, past participle **~ed** endings

6. **tenses**

7. **singular/plural confusion**

8. **sentence structure**

Work with your partner and see if you can identify grammatical mistakes in each of your assignments. Use the eight areas to guide you. You will probably find other types of error as well. Ask your teacher for help if you are not sure whether you have identified an error correctly. This task should take you twenty minutes.

Task 2
Identify areas of grammatical weakness

Take five minutes to make a list of areas of grammar that are problematic for you. Discuss with your partner ways that you can improve your grammar in these areas. Report to the class.

Evaluate your academic language skills

Now that you have finished this textbook, think about how you are now performing and where your strengths and weaknesses lie.

Task 1
Evaluate your academic language skills

Look at the following grading criteria. Answer these questions. Take fifteen minutes to do this with your partner.

1. What overall grade would you give yourself?

2. Which individual sentences reflect your current abilities? (Underline them.)

3. What do you need to do in the future to improve your academic language skills?

Task 2
Discuss your academic language skills

Discuss your self-assessment and action plan with your teacher.

Standard	General expectations of student performance
Excellent	Students are able to produce spoken and written academic texts which are at all times appropriately structured. Students can clearly and concisely explain academic concepts and critically argue for a detailed position. Students always use appropriate academic sources to support their ideas in writing and speaking. They cite and reference correctly at all times. Students demonstrate an ability to fully comprehend and critically interpret spoken and written texts. Written language contains very few, if any, systematic errors in grammar and vocabulary. Spoken language is always comprehensible and fluent.
Good	Students are able to produce spoken and written academic texts which are appropriately structured with only minor errors. Students can almost always clearly and concisely explain academic concepts and almost always critically argue for a detailed position. Students almost always use appropriate academic sources to support their ideas in writing and speaking. They cite and reference correctly with only a few non-systematic errors. Students can comprehend and interpret texts with ease, although they may miss some implied meanings and opinions. Written language is mostly accurate but contains a few systematic errors in complex grammar and vocabulary. Spoken language is mostly comprehensible and fluent.
Satisfactory	Spoken and written academic texts produced by students are sometimes not well-structured but there is some evidence of this ability. Students are sometimes unable to clearly and concisely explain academic concepts. While they can argue for a position, it is not very detailed and tends to be simplistic rather than critical. Students sometimes use sources which are nonacademic and/or not appropriate to support their ideas in writing and speaking. There are some systematic errors in citation and referencing but also evidence of correct systematic use. Students have some difficulty comprehending and critically interpreting texts. They can always understand the main ideas but may miss some of the writer's views and attitudes. Written language is sometimes inaccurate, although errors, when they occur, are more often in complex grammar and vocabulary and there is some evidence of control of simple grammatical structures. Spoken language is generally comprehensible and fluent but at times places strain on the listener. The main ideas are clear.
Pass	Spoken and written academic texts produced by students are often not well-structured but there is some evidence of this ability. Students are often unable to clearly and concisely explain academic concepts and argue for a position. There is some evidence of an ability to explain academic concepts but not to critically argue for a position. Students often use sources which are nonacademic and/or not appropriate to support their ideas in writing and speaking. There are many systematic errors in citation and referencing; however, there is evidence of an understanding of some of the conventions of citation and referencing. Students often have difficulty comprehending and interpreting texts. They can almost always understand the main ideas but often miss some of the writer's views and attitudes. Written language is often inaccurate containing errors in a range of simple and complex grammar and vocabulary. Spoken language is mostly comprehensible. Strain is often placed on the listener and a lack of fluency is noticeable; however, the main ideas are usually clear.
Fail	Productive skills are too limited to be able to successfully carry out spoken and written assessments. Texts are unstructured and unclear. Students are unable to follow and interpret texts. There are language errors in almost every sentence. Spoken language is often incomprehensible. Assessments may not have been attempted or contain plagiarism.